DETROIT PUBLIC LIBRARY

W9-BJZ-695

DETROIT PUBLIC LIBRARY

CHASE BRANCH LIBRARY
17731 W. SEVEN MILE
DETROIT. MICH. 48235

DATE DUE

CHASE BRANCH LIBRARY
17731 W. SEVEN MILE RD.
DETROIT, MI 48235

BC-3

The
TAROT
How to
use and interpret
the cards

Brian Innes

ARCO PUBLISHING COMPANY, INC.
New York

R133.32424
I58t

c.1

JAN '79

Acknowledgments

With the following exceptions, all illustrations
are from the author's collection. Page 20, top
left: Scala – 22, lower right: National
Museum, Naples – 25, bottom right: National
Museum, Naples – 36, bottom: National
Gallery, London – 38, top: Bodleian Library
Filmstrip, MS Douce 188, f. 45 – 48, centre:
Egyptian Museum, Berlin – 50, left: Reims
Cathedral – 59: Phédon Salou – 86: British
Museum

Published 1978 by Arco Publishing
Company, Inc. 219 Park Avenue South,
New York, N.Y. 10003

Copyright © Orbis Publishing, London 1977
All rights reserved
Printed in Italy

**Library of Congress Cataloging in
Publication Data**
Innes, Brian.
The Tarot.

Bibliography: P. 89
1. Tarot. I. Title.
BF1879.T2156   133.3'2424   77-27587
ISBN 0-668-04552-3

CH
Ref.

Contents

1
The origins of playing cards

Nobody can truly say where playing cards have come from. One of the most plausible theories is that they have developed from the same source as the game of chess: the Indian game of *Chaturange* (Four Kings), for instance, has four groups of pieces comprising King, General, Horseman and a phalanx of foot soldiers; and one Chinese card game has the same name as Chinese chess, *Keuma-Paou* (Chariots-Horses-Guns).

Another possibility is that the Chinese, who invented paper money very early, and who also were inveterate gamblers, eventually developed special pieces of paper which, while representing sums of money to be gambled, also represented different aspects of the gambling game.

Without doubt, however, cards have been used since the earliest times for divination. One of the most primitive ways of making decisions was to throw one or more arrows into a circle on the ground, to see which way they pointed; and it is significant that the Korean pack of eighty cards known as *Htou-Tjyen* still bears a stylised arrow on the back of each card.

How cards came to Europe is equally a mystery. It was long believed that they had been brought from the east, either by returning Crusaders or by gypsies, but both these theories would seem to be disproved by the date of the first definite reference to cards, which is 1377–79. We find a German monk named Johannes writing at Brefeld in Switzerland that 'a game called the game of cards has come to us in this year 1377'; and the chronicler Giovanni Covelluzzo,

who wrote his history of the Italian town of Viterbo in 1480, is credited with the statement 'in the year 1379 the game of cards was brought into Viterbo from the country of the Saracens, where it is called *naib*'.

Now, the last crusade began in 1270, and the Christians were finally driven out of Asia Minor in 1291; there were several condemnations of gaming and dicing made during the next hundred years, but without any mention of cards, which seems unlikely if they had really been brought back by the Crusaders. Gypsies, on the other hand, did not appear in Europe until the fifteenth century; they undoubtedly adopted playing cards very quickly, but cards had certainly arrived before them.

The statement of Covelluzzo is particularly attractive, in the light of the fact that cards are known in Spain to this day as *naipes*. The Arabs brought many things to Europe through their occupation of Spain for six centuries, and some scholars believe the word *naib* to be of Arabic origin. There are certain other indications which suggest that cards may well have reached the rest of Europe through Spain, although few Spanish cards earlier than 1600 have survived.

The idea of the different suits is as old as the cards themselves: Korean cards are divided into eight suits, Chinese cards usually into four, and Indian cards into eight – or sometimes into ten, representing the ten incarnations of Vishnu.

There are a wide variety of packs of cards produced in Europe for all sorts of different games, but all comprise four suits. The total

number of cards in the four suits may vary, depending upon the game, between 32 and 56, but each suit will comprise some of the following cards: King, Queen, Knight and Squire or Valet (the 'court' or 'coat' cards), and the complete run of numbered cards from ten down to one (the Ace).

The first European suits, which have remained almost unchanged in Spain and Italy, were Cups, Batons, Swords and Gold Discs. The significance of these particular symbols goes very deep into history. The legend of the Holy Grail, for instance, suggests that these four suits represent the Grail itself, the sacred lance of Longinus that pierced the side of Christ on the cross, the legendary sword of King David, and the paten of the Last Supper. But these four 'Grail Hallows' are at least in part derived from an ancient Celtic tradition, which had survived in Ireland as the Four Treasures: the Cauldron of the Dagda, the Spear of Lug, the Sword of Nuada and the Stone of Fal. The connection between the Stone of Fal, the paten of the Last Supper, and the gold disc of the pack of cards may seem rather tenuous; it appears less so when it is remembered that the equivalent of this suit in a French pack is the *carreau*, or flooring tile – which in its turn has become the diamond of the English pack.

In Italian, the four suits are known as *coppe* (cups), *bastoni* (batons or clubs), spade (swords) and *denari* (coins); and in Spanish as *copas, bastos, espadas,* and *oros* (gold pieces). In the French pack, the symbol for the cup became distorted into a heart shape, *coeur*; the baton into a clover-leaf shape, *tréfle*; the sword into the broader shape of a pike-head, *pique*; and the gold disc was replaced by the *carreau*. These were adopted for the English pack, but in English the names of two suits, spades and clubs, clearly indicate their origin.

In Germany, the earliest cards known have suits of dogs, stags, ducks and falcons; but by 1460 what were to become the traditional suits were already established. Hearts remained the same, but the clover-leaf suffered a further distortion into an acorn, and the pikehead into a leaf; while the gold disc became a little round hawk bell.

One other feature of the 32 – 56 card pack is worthy of mention. From the late fifteenth century onward, the court cards of the French pack have borne the names of legendary or mythical characters. There have been various local variations, but the standard names have been, and still are, as follows:

King of Hearts: Charles
King of Spades: David
King of Diamonds: Caesar
King of Clubs: Alexander
Queen of Hearts: Judith
Queen of Spades: Pallas
Queen of Diamonds: Rachel
Queen of Clubs: Argine
Valet of Hearts: La Hire
Valet of Spades: Hogier
Valet of Diamonds: Hector
Valet of Clubs: Lancelot

In themselves, these names do not tell us very much about the history of playing cards: the kings are named after great military leaders of antiquity, the queens after prototypical female figures, and the valets after famous champions (Ogier the Dane was one of the legendary knights of Charlemagne; La Hire, on the other hand, was one of those who helped Joan of Arc liberate Orleans in 1429). But when we remember the possible connection of the four suits with the four Grail Hallows, the appearance of David as the King of Swords, and of Lancelot as the Valet of Clubs (supposed to represent the lance of Longinus), is significant. What is also important to remember is that each of these characters had a particular symbolism for medieval people; each was held up as an outstanding combination of certain virtues and abilities, and this is why there is no connection of religion, nationality or era, between the king, queen and knave of any suit.

The most remarkable thing about the playing cards we have been considering is that, within two generations of the date of 1377, they had not only spread all over Europe but had attained a standard of design that remained almost unchanged thereafter, even to the present day. Equally remarkable is the fact that another 22 cards were added to the pack, derived from a completely different source, that have also remained virtually unchanged over more than five hundred years. These are the cards that have received most attention from occultists and fortune-tellers alike, and that (not entirely correctly) we call today the Tarot.

Traditional symbols for the four suits of the playing card pack, as reproduced in the first book book to describe the occult significance of the Tarot, Court de Gebelin's *Monde Primitif*. From left to right: cups, rods, swords and *(above)* coins

2
The history of the Tarot

'If one were to let it be announced that there survived to this day an ancient Egyptian work, a book that had escaped the flames which devoured their superb libraries, and which contained, unsullied, their teachings on important matters: everyone, no doubt would be in a hurry to acquaint themselves with such a precious and remarkable book. And if one added that this book was widely distributed throughout much of Europe, and that for many centuries it had been available to everybody, people's surprise would be vastly increased; and would it not reach its highest pitch when they were assured that nobody had ever imagined it to be Egyptian, that it was held to be nothing, that no-one had attempted ever to decipher a single page, and that the fruits of infinite wisdom were regarded as a collection of fantastic pictures without the least significance in themselves? Wouldn't it be thought that one was amusing oneself at the expense of the listeners' credulity? . . . . Nevertheless, it is true: this Egyptian book, sole relic of their superb libraries, survives today. Indeed, it is so common, that no scholar has deigned to concern himself with it; before ourselves, nobody has ever suspected its illustrious origins. This book is composed of 77 or perhaps 78 leaves or pictures, divided into five classes, each presenting objects as varied as they are entertaining and instructive: this book is, in other words, the game of Tarot.'

With these words, the French writer Court de Gebelin began page 365 of the eighth volume of his book *Monde Primitif* in 1781. He was not a particularly eminent author – an obscure Protestant theologian from the South of France, he devoted some ten years to writing his vast pot-pourri of uninformed speculation on the survival of ancient myths, symbols and fragments of primitive tongues – and two-thirds of the way through volume 8 is not the most prominent position in any work, on no matter how fascinating a subject; nevertheless, it is solely for what he had to say about the Tarot that Court de Gebelin is remembered.

Tarot cards were almost unknown in Paris, but Court de Gebelin was familiar with them from his upbringing in the Languedoc, the Mediterranean region adjacent to the Spanish border. He was also aware of their popularity in Germany and Italy, where they were used in a game called *Tarocke* or *Tarocchi*. The pack of cards totalled 78: of these 56 were the standard pack, comprising four suits of 14 cards each, to which were added 22 picture cards or trumps, numbered from 1 to 21 with the last card un-numbered.

According to Court de Gebelin, 'the trumps, numbering 22, represent in general the temporal and spiritual leaders of society, the principles of agriculture, the cardinal virtues, marriage, death and resurrection or the creation; the many tricks of fortune, the wise and the foolish, time which consumes all, etc.. . . . ' As for the suits, he decided that they represented the four classes into which Egyptian society had been divided: the king and military nobility, symbolised by the sword; agriculture, symbolised by the club; the priesthood, symbolised by the cup; and commerce, symbolised by the coin.

He was also struck by the recurrence of the number seven: each suit comprised twice seven cards, and the numbered trumps made three times seven. All these things convinced Court de Gebelin that the cards were undoubtedly of Egyptian origin, and he claimed to be able to discern ancient Egyptian symbolism in the pictorial trumps.

Before we begin to discuss these pictures and what they represent, it is necessary to trace the career of some of the ideas first put forward in *Monde Primitif*.

Among those in Paris who were particularly struck with the ideas of Court de Gebelin was a certain wigmaker named Alliette, who had decided to practise as a fortune-teller, reversing the letters of his name to Etteilla for the purpose. Etteilla welcomed Court de Gebelin's theories, and elaborated upon them, declaring that the Tarot had been written on golden leaves in a temple near Memphis, 171 years after the flood; Hermes Trismegistos had planned the book, which should therefore properly be called *The Book of Thoth*, and it had been executed by seventeen magi working for four years. He even produced his own pack of 78 Tarot cards, which differed markedly in a number of respects from the traditional.

One of Etteilla's other interests was the Qabalah, the ancient Jewish mystical system, which expresses all creation in terms of ten concepts known as *sefiroth*. These ten sefiroth are arranged upon a symbolic Tree of Life: the meditating mystic, as he gains in experience, imagines himself traversing paths from sefiroth to sefiroth, beginning at Malkuth, the earthly kingdom, and finally reaching Kether, the supreme crown. And the total number of paths connecting the ten sefiroth is 22.

The French occultist Eliphas Lévi seized on this fact as proof that the Tarot cards were older, and of more universal significance, than even Court de Gebelin had suggested. Since the Hebrew alphabet contains 22 letters, he succeeded in relating each Tarot trump to a letter of the alphabet

Opposite: Twelve from the fifty cards known as the 'Mantegna' *tarocchi*. Others are illustrated with the individual Tarot cards to which they are related. *Above*: the Magician, as engraved for Court de Gebelin. It is interesting that most of these illustrations, having been produced (presumably) by an amateur engraver, are reversed from left to right; however three – the Wheel of Fortune, Death and the Sun – are correct

The history of the Tarot

From left to right, above: the Woman Pope, the Empress, the Emperor, the Pope, the Lovers and the Chariot; *below*: Justice, the Hermit, the Wheel of Fortune, Fortitude, 'Prudence' and Death. All are from Court de Gebelin, and the transformation of the Hanged Man into the portrait of the prudent man 'who, having put one foot forward, has lifted the other and now stands there examining the ground where he can place it safely' is very striking.

But Court de Gebelin did not explain how this man came to have one foot tethered to a stake

and to one of the 22 paths; and in his first book, *Dogme et Rituel de la Haute Magie*, he promised to make public the original designs from which the popular Tarot cards were derived. Although he described these designs, Lévi himself did not publish them – although the English freemason Kenneth Mackenzie wrote of having seen them in 1861 – and the nearest idea that we have of them is the pack of cards designed by Oswald Wirth to the specifications of Lévi's disciple Stanislas de Guaita, which was eventually made public in 1889. In fact, these cards are little more than a late nineteenth century prettification of the eighteenth century cards described by Court de Gebelin, with the addition of the letters of the Hebrew alphabet.

The next development came from another of Lévi's disciples, a librarian at the Ministry of Public Instruction in Paris named Jean-Baptiste Pitois, who wrote a *History of Magic* under the name of Paul Christian. Attributing his source (entirely without justification) to the ancient Roman philosopher Iamblichus, Christian describes the initiation rites of the Egyptian Mysteries, and the use of 22 paintings along the walls of a subterranean gallery in the Great Pyramid. His descriptions of these paintings are a strongly Egyptianised form of the traditional Tarot trumps, but there is no evidence that they are derived from anything but Christian's imagination, suitably inflamed by Lévi's theories.

After this, variations in Tarot pack design,

and in the interpretations to be attached to the different cards, proliferated thick and fast. A seminal work was the slim volume by the English occultist Macgregor Mathers, which was published in 1888; this was shortly followed by *The Tarot of the Bohemians: Absolute Key to Occult Science*, by the French physician Gerard Encausse, writing under the name of Papus. Then the translator of Papus's book, the Englishman A. E. Waite, designed another very different pack which was executed for him by Pamela Colman Smith. There was a Golden Dawn pack, similar to the Waite pack but with differences of detail; and Aleister Crowley's *Book of Thoth*, painted for him by Frieda Harris.

With the growing interest in the Tarot of the past few years there have been a number of new designs, some attractive, some grotesque. But every new pack introduces details that were not present in the pack described by Court de Gebelin, and which have been added to exemplify some pet theory of the designer. The order of the cards is changed; some cards are discarded and replaced by entirely new ones; often the names of the individual trumps are altered in an attempt to make them conform to a more rigid system.

How 'genuine', however, was Court de Gebelin's pack? and what was its origin? He described each of the trumps, and also illustrated them, and there is no doubt that he was referring to the 22 trumps of the standard eighteenth century pack which is

The history of the Tarot

Right: the Court de Gebelin representation of Temperance. *Far right*: a fine example of a medieval memory image, from Thomas Murner's *Chartiludium logicae* (Strasbourg, 1509), which describes a card game for learning the processes of logic

now known as the 'Marseilles' pack. There are some inconsistencies in the drawings and descriptions in Court de Gebelin's work, but the 'standard' pack can be assumed to be as follows.

I	le Bateleur	The Magician
II	la Papesse	The Female Pope
III	l'Imperatrice	The Empress
IV	l'Empereur	The Emperor
V	le Pape	The Pope
VI	l'Amoureux	The Lovers
VII	le Chariot	The Chariot
VIII	Justice	Justice
IX	l'Ermite	The Hermit
X	la Roue de Fortune	The Wheel of Fortune
XI	la Force	Strength
XII	le Pendu	The Hanged Man
XIII	(untitled: represents Death)	
XIV	Temperance	Temperance
XV	le Diable	The Devil
XVI	la Maison Dieu	The Ruined Tower
XVII	l'Etoille	The Star
XVIII	la Lune	The Moon
XIX	le Soleil	The Sun
XX	le Jugement	(Last) Judgment
XXI	le Monde	The World
(either without number, or numbered 0):		
	le Mat	The Fool

Where do these pictures come from? Of one thing we can be quite sure: their source is not ancient Egypt. When Court de Gebelin published his book in 1781 Egypt was a place of mystery; hieroglyphic writing, in those years before the discovery of the Rosetta stone, appeared incapable of decipherment, and antiquarians were frustrated by the thought that they could never discover the secrets contained in papyri and on steles. It was fashionable to suggest that all the wisdom of the world might be concealed in a tantalising series of pictures that only those initiated into the mysteries could interpret.

In fact, there is plenty of evidence to show that the 22 Tarot trumps are the remnants of a late-medieval instructive card game. Much as we today teach our younger children with table games such as picture dominoes or Scrabble, the rich of the middle ages devised games which exploited the well-known memory images. Before the invention of printing a well-trained memory was essential to an intellectual, and all memory systems were based upon a repertoire of easily recognised images – saints with the symbols of their martyrdom, mythological characters, personifications of the cardinal virtues or of the parts of knowledge (Grammar, Rhetoric, etc). The introduction of printing sounded the death-knell of these memory systems, and it is perhaps no coincidence that the first card games employing memory images appeared almost coincidentally with the invention of printing in Europe.

There are, for instance, the *tarocchi* supposed to have been engraved by the artist Mantegna, which are made up of five sets of ten cards: numbers 1 to 10 represent the orders of society from the beggar to the Pope, numbers 11 to 20 comprise the nine Muses and Apollo, numbers 21 to 30 are the principal parts of knowledge, and numbers 31 to 40 are a rather mixed bag made up of three 'sciences' (astronomy, chronology and cosmology), the four cardinal virtues (temperance, prudence, fortitude and justice) and the three Christian virtues (faith, hope and charity); while numbers 41 to 50 comprise the seven planets, the stellar sphere, the prime mover and the first cause, as required by classical astronomy.

The 'Mantegna' cards seem to be the most complete, in the sense of comprising a range of images to represent just about everything that a fifteenth century educated person might be expected to know, but there are a number of other packs which are much closer in their constitution to today's full Tarot pack. The cards produced in Florence for the game of *minchiate*, for instance, included 42 trumps:

I	The Magician	XVIII	Faith
II	The Grand Duke	XIX	Charity
		XX	Fire
III	The Emperor	XXI	Water
IV	The Empress	XXII	Earth
V	Love	XXIII	Air
VI	Temperance	XXIV	Libra
VII	Fortitude	XXV	Virgo
VIII	Justice	XXVI	Scorpio
IX	The Wheel of Fortune	XXVII	Aries
		XXVIII	Capricorn
X	The Chariot	XXIX	Sagittarius
XI	The Hermit	XXX	Cancer
XII	The Traitor	XXXI	Pisces
XIII	Death	XXXII	Aquarius
XIV	The Devil	XXXIII	Leo
XV	The Tower	XXXIV	Taurus
XVI	Hope	XXXV	Gemini
XVII	Prudence		

The history of the Tarot

Two further examples of medieval memory images, from Johannes Romberch's *Congestiorum Artificiose Memorie* (Venice, 1533) and from *Ars memorandi* (1470). The combination of a statuesque figure with a number of incongruous additions is strikingly like that of the traditional Tarot cards

After these 35 numbered trumps came a further six without numbers:

The Star, The Sun, The Moon, Fame, The World, and The Fool.

At least three other packs of the same period have survived (at least in part), which appear to have contained 22 trumps substantially the same as those in the Marseilles pack. All three are very similar in their graphic style: the trumps are un-numbered, painted in brilliant colours and illuminated with gold and silver leaf on thick pasteboard, and the subjects are recognisably the same as in the Tarot pack.

The first of these packs comprises a surviving 67 cards, of which eleven are trumps. It appears to have been painted sometime between 1428 and 1447 by Marziano da Tortona for Filippo Maria Visconti, duke of Milan, and was handed down in the Visconti family from generation to generation. The trumps are:

The Woman Pope, otherwise identified as
    Religion or Faith
The Empress
The Emperor
The Lovers
The Chariot
Fortitude
Death
The Judgment
The World

and two cards that must be identified as
    Hope and Charity.

Three other packs are known to have been painted in 1484 by Antonio di Cicognara. One was presented to Cardinal Ascanio Sforza, the son of Francesco Sforza and Bianca Maria Visconti (the two families were united in 1432); the two others were presented to the cardinal's sisters, who were nuns at the Augustinian convent in Cremona founded by the Lady Bianca. Exactly what happened to these packs remains a bit of a mystery. Some of the cards certainly were in the possession of the Colleoni family of Bergamo; some are now in the museum at Carrara; some are in the Pierpont Morgan Library in New York; and there are a certain number in the Victoria & Albert Museum in London. At some time, however, they appear to have been mixed up with another pack painted by Bonifacio Bembo; the style is very similar although not identical, but an American bibliographer has contrived to identify a nearly complete pack from these remnants, which is now known as the 'Bembo' or Visconti-Sforza pack.

One other pack has survived in part, which is as old as – maybe even older than – the 'Bembo' pack. There is an entry in the account book of the treasurer to Charles VI of France for the year 1392, recording a payment to the painter Jacquemin Gringonneur for three packs of cards 'in gold and various colours, of several designs, for the amusement of the said king' Seventeen cards survive in the Bibliothèque Nationale that have long been

12

believed to be the original Gringonneur cards, but it is now thought that they are probably fifteenth century, and of Italian origin. They are in a style similar to, although less sophisticated than, the Visconti and Sforza packs. None of the cards is named or numbered, but sixteen of the seventeen are unmistakably trumps:

l'Empereur	la Maison Dieu
le Pape	la Lune
l'Amoureux	le Soleil
le Chariot	le Jugement
Justice	le Monde (wrongly
l'Ermite	identified by all
la Force	commentators as
le Pendu	la Fortune)
la Mort	le Fou
Temperance	

It is clear, then, that the Tarot pack as we possess it today, with its 22 trumps and four suits of 14 cards, is a conglomeration from a variety of sources. It is certainly not, as Court de Gebelin believed, a single compilation of ancient symbolism – but this adds to, rather than detracts from, its value as a means of divination. Over the centuries the users of the Tarot trumps have consciously or unconsciously selected the medieval imagery that has the greatest significance for them, and the designers of the cards have modified their drawings in much the same way. Of course, the designs of some packs have suffered serious degradation in this process, but at their best the traditional packs have a defined strength of character that cannot be improved upon.

After having established the relatively unchanged designs of the 22 Tarot trumps, it is worth recalling that considerable variation is possible. We have dismissed the Etteilla Tarot as an artificial development, but it seems probable that Alliette derived his ideas from some traditional source, even if it were only a judicious blending of Tarot, *tarocchi* and *minchiate*. The Etteilla pack comprises the following cards:

    I Etteilla (The sun's light clearing the clouds)
    II Fire (A bright star above, two children wrestling below)
    III Water (Substantially the same as The Moon)
    IV Air (Substantially the same as The Stars)
    V Earth (Substantially the same as The World)
    VI Day and night
    VII Support and protection (The fifth day of creation: birds and fishes)
    VIII Etteilla (Eve by a tree)
    IX Justice
    X Temperance
    XI Fortitude
    XII Prudence
    XIII Marriage (Similarities to The Lovers)
    XIV The Devil
    XV The Magician
    XVI Judgment
    XVII Death
    XVIII The Capucin (The Hermit)
    XIX The Temple struck by Lightning
    XX The Wheel of Fortune (Fortune, blindfold, stands on her wheel; unusual as a medieval image, this is probably taken from the 'Gringonneur' World)
    XXI The Chariot
LXXVIII The Fool

That Alliette must have had some external inspiration for his designs is shown by a pack of Spanish provenance in the author's possession, which is similar to, but significantly

Left: the Devil and the Ruined Tower, from Court de Gebelin. Although these illustrations are somewhat crudely engraved, they are of value in establishing the Tarot images as they were before occultists had modified them

different from, the Etteilla pack:

I El Caos: La Nada — Chaos:
    Nothingness
II La Luz — Light (The Sun)
III Las Plantas — The Vegetable World
    (The Moon)
IV El Cielo — The Heavens
V El Cielo, el Hombre y los Animales
    Heaven, Man and the Animals
    (design resembles The World)
VI Los Astros — The Stars
VII Las Aves y los Peces — The Birds
    and the Fishes
VIII Descanso o Repos — Rest or
    Repose
IX La Justicia o La Paz — Justice or
    Peace
X La Templanza — Temperance
XI La Fuerza — Fortitude
XII La Prudencia — Prudence
XIII El Gran Patriarca — The Great
    Patriarch (design resembles The
    Lovers)
XIV El Diablo — The Devil
XV El Falso Adivino — The False
    Soothsayer (design resembles The
    Magician)
XVI Juicio Final — The Last Judgment
XVII La Muerte — Death
XVIII El Ermitano — The Hermit
XIX La Destruccion del Templo — The
    Ruined Tower
XX La Rueda de la Fortuna — The
    Wheel of Fortune
XXI Odio Africano: el Despota—The
    Tyrant (design resembles The
    Chariot)
    La Locura o el Alquimista — The
    Fool or the Alchemist

Although the designs of these cards obviously date from the nineteenth century, they retain quite a number of significant medieval symbols, and their relationship to the 'standard' Tarot can be clearly seen.

In Eastern Europe, Tarot trumps are common that bear little or no resemblance to those described in this book. They comprise 21 numbered cards, and one un-numbered. This un-numbered card is the Joker or Fool, in the travelling musician of trump 1 it is possible to guess at the Magician, and the Imperial eagle of the Habsburgs, perched on a cubic stone, can be found on trump 2. But all the cards are double-ended (like modern Italian Tarots) each bearing two scenes of folk-life in the Austro-Hungarian empire, and it is impossible to relate them in any way to the 'traditional' Tarot; neither do they seem to contain any element of medieval iconography. They can be used, as well as any other pack, for divination; but this book will be devoted to the 'traditional' pack and its historical relatives.

Left: some of the cards from the
Florentine game of *minchiate*.
They represent the Ruined
Tower, the Star, the Moon, the
Devil, the Chariot and Death.
Below and far left: the completion
of the Tarot illustrations from
Court de Gebelin's *Monde
Primitif*: the Stars, the Moon,
the Sun, the Last Judgment,
the World and the Fool . . . . . .

15

3
The Tarot and the Qabala

As we have seen, there is no secret wisdom concealed in the symbolism of the Tarot cards; the cards themselves have come down to us as the necessary equipment for a game called *tarok*, and they comprise the 56 cards of a four-suit pack combined with 22 trumps derived from another game called *minchiate*. The secret of the Tarot is what it symbolises for each individual, and those who want to become expert at divination by its use must become familiar with every little detail of each card, so that they know instinctively what the cards represent for them.

The nineteenth century occultists who wrote so many commentaries on the Tarot divided the 22 pictorial trumps from the rest of the pack, but regarded them all as repositories of secrets: they called the former the Major Arcana (from the Latin word *arca*, a chest in which secret things could be stored), and the latter the Minor Arcana. In the next chapter we shall look at the Major

Arcana in detail, describing the images to be found on each card, and outlining the significance that has been attached to each.

Before beginning this survey, it is necessary to go a little deeper into the supposed connection between the Tarot and the Qabala that was suggested by Etteilla and developed by Eliphas Lévi and Papus.

The Qabala is a mystical system which sets out to provide answers to all the questions that confront religious thinkers. Although in principle it is applicable to any religious question, it is essentially Jewish in its derivation, and for its inspiration it relies heavily upon the Hebrew testament. The writers of the chronicles in the Bible made extensive use of word-play, not only in the sense of puns and allusions to similar-sounding words but in what is called *gematria*. This consists in giving numerical values to every letter of the Hebrew alphabet, and then totalling these values to obtain a value for any word made up of various letters. To Christian readers, by far the most familiar example of this is the statement in the Book of Revelations that 666 is 'the number of the Beast'.

The numerical values assigned to the 22 letters of the Hebrew alphabet are established by tradition. As an example of the kind of calculation performed by Qabalists, consider the passage from Genesis xlix:

> The sceptre shall not depart from Judah, nor a lawgiver from between his feet, until Shiloh come; and unto him shall the gathering of the people be.

The phrase IBA ShILH ('until Shiloh come') is totalled as follows:

I	=	10
A	=	2
Sh	=	300
I	=	10
L	=	30
H	=	5
B	=	2
Total		358

Now, the word Messiah, spelt MShICh, comes to the same total:

M	=	40
Sh	=	300
I	=	10
Ch	=	8
Total		358

and this was taken by the Qabalists as showing that the Messiah was prophesied in the passage concerning Shiloh. Moreover, the brazen serpent of Moses (Numbers, xxi, 9) is NaChaSh:

N	=	50
Ch	=	8
Sh	=	300
Total		358

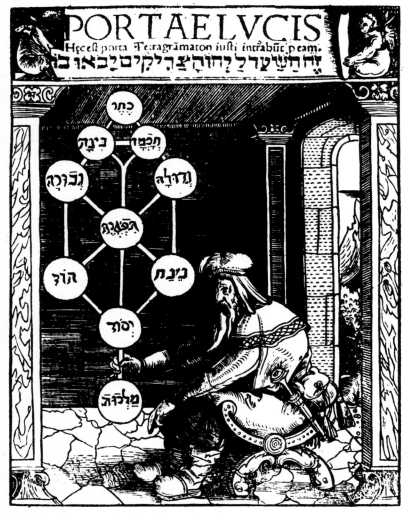

It is clear that this *gematria* is dependent on the peculiarities of Hebrew orthography, in which the vowel sounds are generally omitted; but when works by Jewish mystics began to circulate in Europe in the late Middle Ages they were eagerly seized upon by western magicians, who not only found Christian significance in the Hebrew scriptures and the New Testament, but devised a similar system of their own, based upon the Arabic numerals 1 to 9. This latter system is known as numerology.

The Jewish mystics also developed an ancient concept which sought to explain the integral nature of God and his involvement with every aspect of the universe. This is not the place to go into a detailed description of the mystical *Qabalai*; very briefly, the Qabalists postulated a limitless something, a sort of 'prime cause', which they named the *En-Sof*. The En-Sof came before God the creator, who was manifested as ten lights, the *Sefiroth*, which might be compared to the internal psychic organs of God, and these ten lights were visualised as making up a kind of tree, from the lowest to the highest. At the top was *Kether*, the Crown, and at the bottom, *Malkuth*, the Kingdom.

A very ancient mystical tradition was that of the *Hekhaloth*, or heavenly palaces, through which the mystic must pass on his way to the *Merkabah*, the fiery chariot of God which Ezekiel saw in his vision. The Qabalists soon equated these Hekhaloth with the ten emanations of the Sefiroth, and imagined pathways linking each to each. Altogether, between the ten Sefiroth, there were 22 possible pathways.

It was the recurrence of this figure 22 that led Alliette to propose that the Tarot trumps represented a Qabalistic document. From here it was an easy step to imagine that each card represented one letter of the Sephirothic alphabet and one path up the Sephirothic tree. Eliphas Lévi, and after him Gerard Encausse (Papus), elaborated the theory, and it was taken up by the English occultist Macgregor Mathers. Finally, Aleister Crowley published his *Liber 777* (stolen by him, says the contemporary English writer Ithell Colquhoun, from Mathers), which listed 194 sets of relationships (or 'correspondences') between Hebrew names and numbers of letters, parts of the body, colours, gods of all religions, drugs and perfumes, the planets and signs of the zodiac, and all sorts of other things – including, of course, the cards of the Tarot.

As will be seen in the next chapter, this theory gets off to a good start when card I, the Magician, is equated with the first letter of the Hebrew alphabet, *aleph*. But a similar symbolism cannot be found in any other card of the Tarot trumps, and European occultists soon began to disagree upon which letter should be assigned to which card. Where, for instance, should the Fool be put? Alliette assigned him to card 78, leaving only the first 21 to be allocated 22 letters; Mathers placed

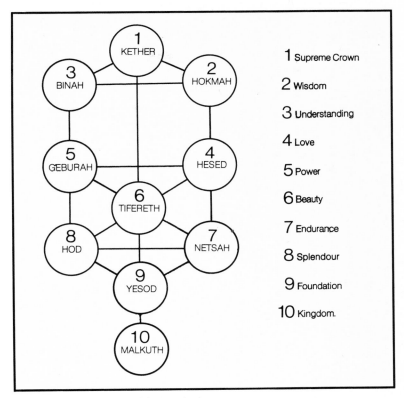

1	Supreme Crown
2	Wisdom
3	Understanding
4	Love
5	Power
6	Beauty
7	Endurance
8	Splendour
9	Foundation
10	Kingdom.

him between cards 20 and 21, equivalent to Sh; Crowley made him the first card. There were similar disagreements upon what the different Hebrew letters were themselves intended to symbolise: the ninth letter, *tet*, represents a roof, says Papus; Mathers (and Crowley) says it is a serpent. Oswald Wirth and Papus added a little serpent to card IX, the Hermit; but Crowley makes *tet* correspond to card VIII, Fortitude. It seems that there is little point in trying to force the Tarot into the Procrustean bed of the Qabala.

Joseph Maxwell, the French Procureur-General, attempted to apply European numerology to the cards. By the rules of numerology, all numbers are eventually reduced to single numerals between 1 and 9; this is done by successively adding the figures making up the number, until a single number is left. Thus, taking the number 358, we get:

$$3+5+8 = 16$$
$$1+6 = 7$$

Maxwell attempted to find significance in the numbers given to the Tarot trumps themselves. Numbers I to IX, of course, remained unchanged; X, by the equation $1+0 = 1$, reduced to unity, and the following cards to 2, 3, etc. One would therefore expect there to be some overt relationship between cards I and X, II and XI, etc; but no such relationship can be found. In fact, this system can be seen to be a numerical system based on the recurrent group of nine, rather than the decimal system of ordinary numbers, or the groups of seven that one might expect to find in the Tarot. As with the Hebrew alphabet, it presents more problems of interpretation than it solves.

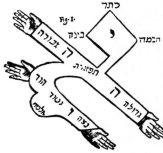

Far left: the Tree of the Sefiroth and (*above left*) its translation into Roman characters. *Above*: qabalistic ideogram of the Hebrew letter *aleph*. The posture of the hands is reminiscent of that of the hands of the Magician, lending somewhat specious support to the suggestion that the Tarot is linked to the letters of the Hebrew alphabet

4
The significance of the Tarot trumps

In the chapter that follows, the images of the Tarot trumps are described, and their significance discussed. Many designs of Tarot pack are available nowadays, some of which have no connection whatsoever with the designs of the past. The packs described in this book are of three types:
(1) Packs of historical importance, which survive in museums and private collections, seldom complete.
(2) Packs of 'traditional' design, manufactured commercially by concerns which, in most cases, have made packs to the same design for two centuries or more.
(3) Packs designed by late-nineteenth and early-twentieth century occultists.
Specifically, the following are described:

Packs of historical importance:
The 'Gringonneur' pack, originally believed to be late fourteenth century French, but now thought to be fifteenth century Italian: Bibliothèque National, Paris
The so-called 'Bembo' pack described in *The Tarot Cards Painted by Bembo* (Gertrude Moakley, New York Public Library). These cards are to be found, some in the Pierpont Morgan Library, New York, and some in the Accademia Carrara, Bergamo. A modern reproduction set has been published. The 'da Tortona' cards, property of the Visconti family, described in the *Burlington Magazine*, 1903, were apparently lost during World War II
The 'Mantegna' *tarocchi*, specimens of which are owned by several different museums
Minchiate cards of various packs; the British Museum has an outstanding collection

Traditional packs:
The 'Tarot of Marseille' published by B. P. Grimaud in France
The Swiss 1JJ pack published by Müller in Switzerland
The pack designed by Claude Burdel, 1751, now redrawn and published by Müller
Italian double-headed pack, published by Modiano

Occultists' packs:
Pack described by Jean-Baptiste Pitois in *History and Practice of Magic*
Pack designed by Oswald Wirth, recently republished in its original coloration as companion to *The Wisdom of the Tarot* by Elisabeth Haich
Pack designed by A. E. Waite, and executed by Pamela Coleman Smith

The first thing that you must do is buy a full pack of Tarot cards. Familiarise yourself with every detail, by laying out the cards in small groups, studying each group, and deciding for yourself what significance each card has for you. You must learn to read them like the letters of the alphabet. But just as different alphabets – in Greek or Russian, for instance – have different letters, so each design of Tarot pack has certain meanings that were incorporated in it by its designer. There are the traditional meanings, which carry forward into every modern pack, and there are the particular significations of newer packs like the Etteilla or the Waite. By comparing these meanings, and understanding the source of the Tarot images, you will gradually build up a vast vocabulary of interpretation.

Full-page illustrations on the following pages set out representative cards from packs in the author's collection. In each case the order is as follows. *Left*: 'Bembo' pack, published in facsimile by US Games Systems. *Top centre*: 'Swiss' 1JJ pack published by Müller. *Top right*: Oswald Wirth pack, published in facsimile by Allen & Unwin. *Centre*: Italian modern pack published by Modiano. *Right centre*: 'Spanish' pack. *Centre bottom*: 'Ancien Tarot de Marseille' published by Grimaud. *Bottom right*: A. E. Waite pack, published by Rider & Co. Where appropriate, cards from the *tarocchi* have been included, *lower left*. *Above*: the Magician as described by Pitois

I The Magician
(French: *le Bateleur*   Italian: *il Bagatto*   German: *der Gaukler*)

A man wearing a broad-brimmed hat stands behind a table, on which are various pieces of the conjuror's equipment, such as dice, balls and cups. In some packs there appears to be a glue-kettle on the table, which has led some people to interpret this figure as a country craftsman, the other implements being perhaps a cobbler's knife and awl. In *minchiate* packs, the magician seems to be demonstrating a card trick to a man and a woman, who stand one behind each shoulder; in the 'Bembo' pack he is seated. Generally he holds a short wand in his left hand,

and a small ball in his right.

Wirth followed the traditional designs quite closely, but the implements on the table are replaced by chalice, sword and gold disc, and the conjuror's wand is increased in length.

Pitois describes the figure as 'the Magus, the type of the perfect man . . . he wears a white robe, his belt is a serpent biting its tail . . . The Magus holds in his right hand a golden sceptre; the index finger of his left hand points to the ground . . .' In front of the Magus, on a cubic stone, are a chalice, a

LE BATELEUR

1   LE BATELEVR

IL BAGATTO

1 Diritto: IL RE THOT

Aleph

EL CAOS

LA NADA

1 Rovescio: IL CONSULTANTE

ARTIXAN ·III·

THE MAGICIAN

THE MAGICIAN.

Below: Hermes Trismegistos, in an inlaid pavement in Siena cathedral. He is described in the inscription as the 'contemporary of Moses'

sword and a golden coin.

The Waite pack pursues this concept, but the cubic stone is once more a table, and on it are all four of the symbols of the suits. The magus is bareheaded, with a gold band about his brow, but above his head the curly shape of the hat brim has been turned into the mathematical figure known as a lemniscate, the symbol for infinity, and roses and lilies bloom around him.

Interpretation: One of the grounds for controversy between different interpreters of the Tarot is whether the Fool – sometimes unnumbered, sometimes numbered 0 – should be considered as the first or last card of the 22. This will be discussed in detail when this card is described; but it will be clear that there are considerable problems for the qabalists. If the cards of the Tarot are to be related to the letters of the Hebrew alphabet, is the Magician *aleph* or *beth*? Most modern occultists, taking their lead from the esoteric traditions represented by the Golden Dawn, assign *beth* to this card; but Lévi, and after him Wirth and Papus, claimed to see the shape of the letter *aleph* in the poise of the magician's body and his arms.

What all are agreed, however, is that the Magician is the Egyptian god Thoth, or Tehuti, who was known to the Greeks as Hermes Trismegistos, 'thrice-great Hermes'. According to the Egyptian myth, Thoth was the god of all knowledge and the inventor of writing; medieval Christians believed him to have been a historical personage, of an age and standing with Moses and Zoroaster, and the possessor of all the secrets of the universe. Hermes is Mercury, messenger of the gods, patron of thieves and mountebanks, and so the simple conjuror that we see in the Tarot may well be Hermes in disguise.

This, like all the Tarot images, is an ambiguous one. It is man in search of knowledge but it is also the elusive source of that knowledge; in the Etteilla pack, card number 1 portrays creation in the void, but it signifies the man who is seeking an answer. Obviously its interpretation depends not only on the question being asked, but upon the relationship between this card and those around it.

One stands for God, and for man, and for the erect phallus. And infinity, like a figure 8 on its side, may represent the testicles; or should we see that broadbrimmed hat as the hat of the pilgrim, the seeker after truth?

II The Woman Pope

(French: *la Papesse*   Italian: *la Papessa*   German: *die Päpstin*)

A seated woman, wearing simple robes, but with the triple crown of the papacy. She carries an open book on her lap. The story of the woman pope can be traced back to 1282, when it appeared in two rather different forms. The legend of Pope Joan was reported in that year by Martin Polonus: according to this, a woman disguised as a man under the name of John Anglus was elected pope after the death of Leo IV (about 855 AD). She was eventually discovered after a period of two years, five months and four days, when she was found to be pregnant. The legend became very popular, although historical record shows that it is no more than a legend: it is known that only a month and a half elapsed between the death of Leo IV and the consecration of Benedict III.

The other story has some foundation in truth, as well as a direct connection with one of the earliest Tarot packs. The founder of an Italian religious sect, the Guglielmites, was Guglielma of Bohemia, and after her death in 1282 the rumour spread that she was to be resurrected in 1300 and usher in a new age in which women should be popes. Sister Manfreda Visconti was elected by the Guglielmites to be their papess, but was burnt at the stake in 1300, and is commemorated in one of the packs made for the Visconti family.

Tarot packs produced in Switzerland and southern France during the eighteenth century frequently replaced the Woman Pope by Juno, with her peacock, which symbolises immortality and the resurrection.

Oswald Wirth rather let his imagination run riot in his design for this card: the subject is still a seated figure wearing a triple crown, and in her left hand Wirth put the keys of St Peter, but the top of the crown is a crescent moon, the seat is a winged lion, and the book bears the Chinese *yin-yang* symbol on its cover.

In the Wirth pack this card is still called la Papesse, but the definitely non-Christian elements reflect the tendency to give this card another name, that of the High Priestess. This derives originally from Court de Gebelin, and was developed by Pitois, who described this figure as 'The Door of the Occult Sanctuary'. A woman is seated on the threshold of the temple of Isis, between a red and a black column. She wears a tiara surmounted by a crescent moon, and on her breast a solar cross. On her knees is an opened book.

The Waite pack, and several others that follow it more or less closely, conforms to this description, except that the crown takes on a very different shape, the crescent moon is placed below the priestess's foot, and the book bears the word 'Tora'. This is a transliteration of the Hebrew for 'law', but it is also an anagram of the letters 'taro'.

Interpretation: This is a card of knowledge, but of hidden knowledge; it represents the way in which understanding may be obtained intuitively rather than by enquiry. If we try to put ourselves in the position of medieval people interpreting this image, we can see

Above: the Woman Pope identified as the priestess of Isis, as described by Pitois

JUNON.

2   LA PAPESSE

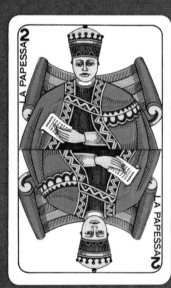

2 Diritto: OSIRIDE O LA GLORIA

2   Beth

LA LUZ

2 Rovescio: FUOCO - COLLERA

THE HIGH PRIESTESS

THE HIGH PRIESTESS

Below: an unusual deviation from the traditional. The Spanish Captain, from an eighteenth century Belgian pack

that for them it represented the dangerous nature of secret knowledge. This enigmatic woman holds the keys of the kingdom and the book of the law, but she is not all that she seems: a woman disguised as the pope is both a sacrilege and an attack upon established order, yet at the same time she represents freedom and progress.

We must not forget her significance as the high priestess, perhaps of Isis; or as Juno or Hera, the queen of heaven – the name of Pope Joan herself is an anglicised form of Juno. For the Greeks identified Isis with Hera; and when Hera, alone and in secret, conceived and produced a child, it was 'not a son who resembled gods or men, but the frightful, the terrible Typhon, scourge of mankind'. So must medieval man have thought of the child that Pope Joan conceived – indeed, perhaps the whole legend is a distorted memory of the myth of Hera, who herself wore a high cylindrical crown.

This card, then, represents a strongly feminine principle. It represents intuition, inspiration, the subconscious memory, perhaps also divination and prophecy. In certain contexts it is a subversive influence; and in detrimental situations it may signify emotional instability or lack of foresight.

III The Empress

(French: *l'Impératrice*   Italian: *l'Imperatrice*   German: *die Herrscherin*)

A fair-haired young woman wearing a crown is seated on a throne. In one hand, generally her left, she holds a sceptre supported by her shoulder, while her right arm nurses a shield bearing an imperial eagle. In some packs she has no shield and carries a spindle-shaped rod in her right hand.

The Wirth design is similar to the traditional designs, but the high back of the Empress's throne has been changed into an angel's wings, her head is surrounded with a halo of nine stars, and her left foot is on an inverted crescent.

In Pitois' description this card is a woman seated at the centre of a blazing sun, and crowned with twelve stars. She carries a sceptre, and on her other hand an eagle, and the moon is beneath her feet.

For Waite, this card was still the Empress, but she also reveals some of the attributes of Ceres or Demeter. Ripe wheat fills the foreground of the card; her shield, which stands by her feet, is heart-shaped and bears the symbol for Venus. She holds her sceptre in her right hand above her shoulder, and her crown is a diadem of twelve stars.

Interpretation: After the French Revolution, packs of cards were deprived of their royal connotations, and the name given to the Empress was *la Grande Mère* – which means, not 'grandmother' but Great Mother. It seems that even as late as the end of the eighteenth century, cardmakers were aware of an ancient tradition that this card really represents the Great Goddess of antiquity.

Demeter, who was known to the Romans as Ceres, was the goddess of the Eleusinian mysteries; she represented the fertility of the earth, and she was often portrayed seated on her throne, crowned with ears of corn and holding a sceptre in her hand. In Arcadia, she was given a dove in one hand, and it is perhaps significant that the *minchiate* pack represents the Empress holding in one hand an orb with something very like a dove on top of it, and in the other a sceptre topped with what looks like an ear of corn.

Where the Woman Pope represented an intellectual aspect of the feminine principle, the Empress may be interpreted as the body of woman, warm, yielding and maternal. In place of the hidden wisdom of the previous card, she offers human understanding and generous sensuality. She is the vegetable world, beauty and happiness – but perhaps with a hint of over-ripeness, even decadence. Deprived of the fire of intellect, she may sink into luxurious idleness, smothered by the richness that she herself has engendered.

Pitois' identification of this card as Isis-Urania is distinctly odd, since Urania was the muse of astronomy, and could hardly be coupled with the most important of the Egyptian goddesses. In any case, as we have seen, the connection between Isis and the Woman Pope is very much stronger. In fact, Pitois' description sounds much more like the goddess known as Ishtar to the Babylonians, Ashtoreth to the Hebrews, and Astarte to the Greeks; and although the Greeks identified Astarte with Aphrodite, her cult was in fact very similar to that of Demeter.

Above: Isis-Urania as described by Pitois. *Right*: statue of the goddess Demeter enthroned, from the National Museum, Naples. By Roman times, Demeter was largely identified with Cybele, the lover of Attis, who is represented in the Tarot by the Hanged Man

L'IMPERATRICE

3 L'IMPERATRICE

THE EMPRESS

THE EMPRESS.

L'EMPEREUR

L'EMPEREVR

4 Diritto: RIFIUTO - SPOGLIAZIONE

EL CIELO

4 Daleth

4 Rovescio: INTELLIGENZA

IMPERATOR·VIIII·

THE EMPEROR

THE EMPEROR.

IV The Emperor

(French: *l'Empereur*   Italian: *l'Imperatore*   German: *der Herrscher*)

Here is an image that has changed very little in the past six hundred years. A crowned man sits in a chair, facing to his right. In his right hand he holds a sceptre, sometimes of an unusual shape, and by his feet is a shield bearing, like that of the Empress, an eagle.

This is the first surviving card in the 'Gringonneur' pack, and the subject is recognisably the same. In addition to his sceptre, the Emperor holds an orb in his left hand; and in place of the shield he is attended by two kneeling boys. Apart from these small differences the card is very similar to that described by Court de Gebelin nearly 400 years later. In the da Tortona pack, however, the Emperor (who is perhaps Frederick III of the Germans) faces directly outward, with two boys behind him and two more kneeling at his feet. The 'Bembo' card is rather different: the Emperor is turned to his left, and there are no attendants.

Oswald Wirth kept closely to the 'traditional' eighteenth century packs, even to the extent of following the strange helmet-like shape of the Emperor's crown; his only major change was in seating the Emperor on a cubic stone decorated with the imperial eagle, rather than a throne with a shield in front of it. He followed, but in a subdued way, the unnatural crossing of the legs in the traditional packs: in these, the Emperor's legs make a shape like the figure 4. The legs of Wirth's Emperor seem almost naturally crossed but Papus, in what purports to be a reproduction of Wirth's design, exaggerates the 4 even further. The significance of this gesture is that it reappears in two other cards.

Pitois calls this card 'The Cubic Stone'. A man wearing a helmet surmounted by a crown is seated on a cubic stone. 'His right hand holds a sceptre, and his right leg is bent and rests on the other in the form of a cross. . . .'

As for Waite, his Emperor sits four-square facing out from the card, on a throne decorated with rams' heads. In his left hand he holds an orb without a cross, and in his right a sceptre topped with the crux ansata. His legs are not crossed.

Interpretation: There is no doubt what the meaning of this card was in medieval times: the Emperor represented temporal power, fatherly protection, strength and leadership. Of course, he also represented the repressive power of the ruling class, and after the French Revolution he was replaced for some time by a figure named, by analogy with the Empress, *le Grande Père*. But this Great Father is not Zeus (Jupiter), any more than the Empress is Hera (Juno); this, the god of plenty and of civilisation, is Dionysos. A bas-relief of Dionysos from the Roman city of Herculaneum makes this very clear: the

Above: the Cubic Stone described by Pitois. *Left*; the first surviving card of the 'Gringonneur' pack. The boy attendants appear only in this and the da Tortona pack. *Below*: relief of Dionysos from Herculaneum

pose on the throne is identical, he holds a sceptre (tipped probably with a pinecone), and his legs are crossed in exactly the same peculiar way as in the traditional Tarot card.

Although we tend to think of Dionysos, whom the Romans called Bacchus, as the god of wine and festivity, in the Orphic religion he finally became, in the words of Plutarch, 'the god who is destroyed, who disappears, who relinquishes life and then is born again'.

We may think of this card as representing the principle of everlasting life, the breath that God breathed into the clay when he made man, the divine inspiration that causes some to rise above the rest. It is the spirit of renewal; it is the idea of persistence in the face of continuing opposition.

So, although this may be the spirit that makes men and women leaders, or captains of industry, it is also the spirit that fills great artists, mystics and saints. It is a source of energy and a source of power; it initiates action, and it then keeps it in continuing motion.

This card is the counterpart to the Empress: masculine as she is feminine, independent as she is all-embracing, creative as she is interpretative.

JUPITER.

5   LE PAPE   7

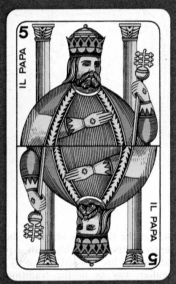

5 Diritto: FELICITA'

He

EL
CIELO   y los
EL   ANI-
HOMBRE   MALES

5 He

5 Rovescio: MISERIA

E   ·PAPA·X·   ·10·

THE POPE

THE HIEROPHANT

V The Pope

(French: *le Pape*   Italian: *il Papa*   German: *der Papst*)

There is no reason to suppose that this card, in medieval packs, symbolised anything other than the Pope: the same subject occurs in the *tarocchi*, and possibly in *minchiate* packs. Without doubt, this card in the 'Gringonneur' pack represents the Pope: in full papal robes, he sits clutching the keys of St Peter, with a cardinal sitting each side of him. In the 'Bembo' pack, he raises his right hand in benediction.

In the 'traditional' designs, this figure is even more clearly the Pope. He wears the triple papal crown, and carries the triple-barred papal cross upright in his left hand. Before him kneel two or three figures with tonsured heads, whom he appears to be blessing.

As with the Woman Pope this figure, in the Swiss and southern French packs, is replaced by Zeus or Jupiter. In the *tarocchi* Jupiter has his own card: he sits, dressed as a crowned king, with an arrow-like thunderbolt in his right hand, and with his eagle close at hand. Card V in those Tarot packs that replace the Pope is very similar to this *tarocchi* Jupiter.

From Court de Gebelin on, writers have identified this card as the Hierophant, the high priest of the Eleusinian mysteries. In the sense that the Christian mystery took over from the mystery of Eleusis, and the Pope is its high priest, this identification seems thoroughly justified. As Pitois put it: 'This prince of occult doctrine is seated between two columns of the sanctuary. He is leaning on a cross with three horizontals, and describes with the index finger of his right hand the sign of silence on his breast. At his feet two men have prostrated themselves....'

Oswald Wirth, on the other hand, portrayed a story-book Pope, very similar to the traditional representation. Two monks kneel before him, and he blesses them with his right hand. There are none of the extra occult symbols that Wirth put into so many of his Tarot cards.

Waite, also, restrained himself in the design of this card. His Hierophant sits on the throne, with two kneeling monks before him. His right hand is raised in benediction, and his left holds the triple cross. The crossed keys of St Peter are at his feet.

Interpretation: This card is the male counterpart of card II, the Woman Pope. Where she represents intuition, the Pope represents analytical intelligence. The keys that he holds are the keys of knowledge, the blessing he bestows is the blessing of understanding.

At Memphis, the ancient capital of Egypt, the bull Apis was worshipped as a symbol of divine procreativity. When each Apis died, he was identified with Osiris, and in due course the cult of Oserapis developed. Alexandria was established by the Greeks in

Above: the 'prince of occult doctrine' described by Pitois. *Left*: the 'Gringonneur' Pope with his two cardinals. *Far left*: card V in the 'Spanish' pack closely resembles the World in the traditional Tarot

the Nile delta in the fourth century BC, and the chief deity of the place became Serapis, adopted by the Greeks from the Egyptian Oserapis. A magnificent temple was built for the new god, where his statue represented him as a bearded and throned figure. similar to Zeus. To symbolise his connections with the underworld (of which Osiris was king), he was attended by the three-headed dog Cerberus. It seems very likely that this may be the origin of the heads of the three figures kneeling before the Pope; it is also significant that, at the time the first Tarot cards were designed, the badge of the Pope, Alexander Borgia, was a bull.

As Zeus or Jupiter, then, the Pope represents natural law and justice; as Osiris, or his priest, he represents redemption; as Serapis he represents healing. He is the adviser, the confessor, the confidant. But he may also symbolise the repressive aspects of a too rigid orthodoxy. Taking it all in all, therefore, we may identify the Pope with the firm foundation of our lives, the laws of the universe which may not easily be transgressed; but it is essential that we should understand how those laws have been framed.

L'AMOUREUX.

6 L'AMOVREVX 7

GLI AMANTI

6 Diritto: LA NOTTE

6 Vau

LOS ASTROS

6 Rovescio: IL GIORNO

VENVS XXXXIII

VI

THE LOVER

VI

THE LOVERS.

VI The Lover, or The Lovers

(French: *l'Amoureux*   Italian: *gli Amanti*   German: *die Liebenden*)

The first five cards of the Tarot pack appear to be well-defined images whose significance goes back into antiquity without much change, but this sixth card begins to show some of the confusion between different images that gradually crept in as the cards were copied from one cardmaker to another. At least three separate images have been incorporated into the traditional card, and account for its evident ambiguity.

These are (1) the pair or pairs of lovers strolling and talking together, while Cupid (or some cherubs) aims his darts from a cloud above; (2) the legend of the Judgment of Paris, unable to make up his mind between the charms of Hera, Athene and Aphrodite; and (3) the man unable to make his choice between virtue and vice, sometimes symbolised in the middle ages as the Choice of Hercules.

In the traditional design a single Cupid aims his arrow at a young man who has a woman at each side; one of these figures might be considered less good-looking than the other, but it is difficult to tell. The cloud from which Cupid leans has been transformed into a glorious sun.

The eighteenth century Swiss card is very similar to the traditional in its graphic grouping, but the three figures comprise a pair of lovers observed sardonically by an elderly man leaning on a staff.

There is little doubt that the original subject of this card was 'The Lovers'. The 'Gringonneur' card shows no less than three pairs promenading, while two cherubs aim their arrows; the da Tortona pack shows a single pair – presumed to be Duke Filippo Maria Visconti and his first wife, Beatrice di Tenda – in front of a magnificent pavilion over which hovers a blindfolded Cupid; the 'Bembo' card is similar, except that the Cupid is on a pedestal and there is no pavilion, and the loving pair are believed to be Francesco Sforza and Bianca Maria Visconti; and the *minchiate* cards feature a crowned prince kneeling at a girl's feet beneath a menacing arrow that Cupid is just about to loose. The *tarocchi*, on the other hand, show us Venus bathing, attended by her handmaidens; blindfolded Cupid stands to one side, with his bow, and overhead fly Venus's doves.

Oswald Wirth revealed himself strongly in favour of the image of the man unable to make up his mind: his young lover stands undecided between two beautiful girls, one a princess with 'a small but costly crown', the other ragged, barefooted, with flowers in her hair.

Pitois opts for the third concept: he calls this card 'The Two Roads'. It shows, he says, a man standing motionless at a crossroads, with his arms crossed on his breast. Two women personifying virtue (with a

Left: the 'Gringonneur' portrayal of the Lovers shows a typical courtly scene of the fifteenth century. *Below*: Pitois calls this card 'The Two Roads'

fillet of gold round her head) and vice (crowned with vineleaves) point out the two ways to him. 'Above and behind this group the genius of Justice, borne on a nimbus of blazing light, is drawing his bow and directs the arrows of punishment at vice.'

Waite's card for The Lovers makes some kind of combination of concepts 1 and 3. It shows Adam and Eve: Eve stands in front of the Tree of Knowledge of Good and Evil, round which is wound the snake; Adam stands before a tree of flames. Behind them an angel raises his arms in benediction.

Interpretation. The most important feature of this card is the element of choice: this is implied even in the earliest form of the card, because the lovers have undoubtedly chosen each other, even if they are not represented at the actual moment of choosing. The nature of the choice to be made will, of course, depend upon the context in which the card is found. In spite of the sexual nature of the imagery, you must not assume that the question is necessarily one of love or marriage. It may be connected with any aspect of your life.

The outcome of choice is decision, followed by commitment. Some commentators have interpreted the traditional card of The Lovers as a young man and woman swearing their vows before an elder. Certainly, this card demands an end to vacillation; whoever receives it when cards are read must make up his or her mind to undertake a specific course of action.

At the same time, the card emphasises the difficulty of making the correct decision. Cupid's arrow points menacingly, like a bolt from heaven ready to fall upon anybody who takes a wrong step. Poor Paris! whichever goddess he chose (and he chose Aphrodite) he made an enemy of each of the others. The choice may lie between love and all the passions of the body, or the ascetic life of the intellectual. Which is the vice and which is the virtue? this is the question that many find impossible to answer.

VII The Chariot

(French: *le Chariot*   Italian: *il Carro*   German: *der Wagen*)

Here is an image that occurs in all the different sources we have been considering: in the *tarocchi*, in the *minchiate* cards, and in the earliest Tarots. In the *tarocchi* it is the chariot of Mars: it does not seem to be drawn by anything, and Mars sits on a sort of plinth, his sword over his right shoulder and a dog (one of the dogs of war?) at his feet. In the *minchiate* a naked female figure rides on the top of a wagon, which is drawn by two horses, one of them ridden by a groom. She holds a wide ribbon behind her shoulders with the words 'Viva Viva'.

The image is essentially the same in the da Tortona and 'Bembo' packs; but the woman is richly dressed and crowned and carries an imperial orb in her hand. Two white horses draw the car, and in the 'Bembo' pack there is no outrider. In the 'Gringonneur' pack the figure is that of a soldier holding a battleaxe. The most important feature of this card, however, is that it is coming straight towards us, and the artist, unable to cope with the problem of perspective, has drawn the two horses pulling in divergent directions. This feature was copied in many later packs.

The traditional packs follow this line – indeed, perspective has been evaded further and the hindquarters of the horses are invisible, while the wheels on each side are turned even further outward. The principal difference is that the triumphal car itself appears much more like that of Mars. A crowned king stands inside it under a draped canopy, showing only the upper part of his body and carrying a sceptre in his right hand. In Swiss Tarots the upper part of this image has become entirely divorced from the rest: the upper half of the card portrays the king (with the sceptre in his left hand); the lower part contains a complete carriage drawn by two horses.

The Oswald Wirth design is similar to the traditional, but there is a very significant difference: the chariot is drawn by a white and a black sphinx. These, according to Pitois, are respectively Good and Evil – 'the one conquered, the other vanquished'.

Pitois described this card in some detail. It is 'The Chariot of Osiris', and represents a war chariot, square in shape, with a starred

Above: the 'Chariot of Osiris' as described by Pitois. *Right*: the fiery chariot of Ezekiel's vision, as illustrated in the 'Bear' Bible. *Further right*: the triumphal chariot of military power, from the 'Gringonneur' pack

VII

LE CHARIOT

7　LE CHARIOT　7

IL CARRO 7

IL CARRO 7

7 Diritto: APPOGGIO

7 Zain

LAS AVES
Y
LOS PECES

7 Rovescio: PROTEZIONE

A · MARTE · XXXXV · 4

VII

THE CHARIOT

VII

THE CHARIOT.

LA JUSTICE

8 LA JVSTICE ਜ

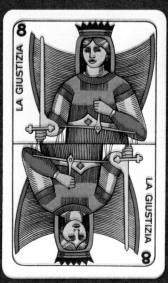

LA GIUSTIZIA

LA GIUSTIZIA

8 Diritto: LA VIRTU'

8 Heth

DESCANSO ó REPOSO

Heth 8

8 Rovescio: LA CONSULTANTE

B ·IVSTICIA XXXVII· 37

VIII

JUSTICE

XI

JUSTICE .

baldaquin held up by four columns. The 'armed conqueror' carries a sceptre and a sword, and he is crowned with a fillet of gold decorated at five points by groups of three pentagrams.

Waite's design follows the same lines as Wirth and Pitois, but the canopy is smaller than on any other card, to leave room for the walls and towers of a city to be visible behind the chariot.

Interpretation. The chariot is a triumphal one, in which a military conqueror is paraded through the streets to celebrate his success. Indeed, it is this card that has given the word 'trump' to the English language, derived directly from the word 'triumph'. It is the war-chariot of Mars, the Indian *juggernaut*, clearing everyone before it or crushing them beneath its wheels.

But it is also the fiery chariot of Ezekiel's vision, the *merkabah* or Throne Chariot of God that Jewish mystics believed they could attain in trance. The way by which they ascended, through the heavenly halls of the *hekhaloth*, was very like the ascent of the sefirothic tree.

The Chariot, then, represents achievement, success, ultimate victory; and not only in a material but also in a spiritual sense. But it is very important to take care that one is not carried away by this success, running down and destroying everything that lies in the chariot's path; eventually the chariot may itself be overturned, and what began in triumph will end in defeat – perhaps, in spiritual destruction.

VIII Justice

(French: *la Justice* Italian: *la Giustizia* German: *die Gerechtigkeit*)

Four cardinal virtues were recognised in antiquity: Justice, Fortitude, Temperance and Prudence. To these, Christians added Faith, Hope and Charity. All seven were represented in the *minchiate* cards, but strangely the grouping was changed, so that cards numbered VI to VIII represented Temperance, Fortitude and Justice respectively, while Prudence was grouped with the Christian virtues as cards XVI to XIX. The Tarot pack retains Justice, Fortitude, and Temperance, numbered VIII, XI and XIV respectively.

This figure is once again a simple medieval image. The female Justice, wearing a headdress which is not a crown but some sort of mobcap (or perhaps a star-shaped halo), sits upon a throne holding a sword in her right hand and a pair of scales in her left. The only variants on this are that, in the *minchiate* pack, these objects are in the opposite hands, while the Swiss Tarot has Justice in some form of armour, standing.

For various reasons, principally because he wanted to relate the Tarot cards in the right order to the signs of the zodiac, Macgregor Mathers decided to number this card XI rather than VIII, transposing it with Fortitude. This order was adopted by the Golden Dawn: Waite, therefore, and Crowley and other occultists who follow the same persuasion, all have Justice as the eleventh card.

Wirth, however, gave Justice the number VIII, and the figure he designed did not differ significantly from the traditional. Even Pitois' description, supposed to be of an ancient Egyptian mural, is almost identical. He called the card 'Themis': 'a woman seated on a throne wearing a crown armed with spear points: she holds in her right hand an upward-pointing sword and in the left a pair of scales.'

Waite, also, adhered closely to the traditional form, the only major difference being that his Justice wears a square-cut crown.

Interpretation: Themis, whom Pitois identifies with this card, was the ancient Greek goddess of justice and good advice, but she was also the interpreter of the will of the gods and had the gift of delivering oracles.

The Card of Justice, therefore, can be taken to represent the careful weighing of advice, or the equilibrium that can result

The figure of Justice changes very little from pack to pack; from the 'Gringonneur' (*left*) to Pitois' 'Themis' (*above*). Note, however, that the Waite pack (*below, left*) has this card numbered XI, and Justice in the 'Spanish' pack is numbered VIIII

L'ERMITE

L'ERMITE

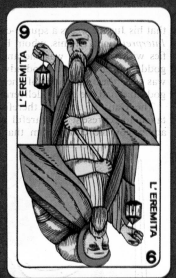

9 Diritto: LA GIUSTIZIA

9 Teth

LA JUSTICIA
ó LA PAZ

9 Teth

9 Rovescio: DISACCORDO

A · SATVRNO · XXXXVII · 47

VIIII

THE HERMIT

THE HERMIT.

when all forces are balanced one against another; but it can also advise us to weigh a situation very carefully before committing ourselves to an irrevocable course of action. By development from this it can be seen as a card that symbolises the way in which mankind can take a hand in controlling its fate, rather than submit to blind chance. At the same time it warns us that adherence to nothing but the most rigorous logic can lead to bigotry, narrow-mindedness and excessive severity.

IX The Hermit

(French: *l'Ermite*   Italian: *l'Eremita*   German: *der Weise*)

Here is another medieval image that is hardly changed from pack to pack. In the 'Bembo' and 'Gringonneur' Tarots, and in the *minchiate* pack, the figure is a bearded hunchback in monkish robes carrying an hourglass. In the *minchiate*, he walks with crutches, and the hourglass is carried on his hump; the head of a sitting deer can be seen beyond him. It seems likely that this figure is connected with that of Saturn, in the character of Kronos with his hourglass and scythe, which occurs in the *tarocchi*.

In its traditional form, this card shows a man in a hooded cloak walking towards his right; he carries a lantern in his right hand and a walking stick in his left. He may be known alternatively as the Capucin.

Oswald Wirth's design was substantially the same; but where all the traditional packs show the Hermit with his hood on his back, Wirth's wears his hood up. He is accompanied by a small snake, which is reared up beside him; this was added by Wirth presumably to give colour to the proposal by Lévi that this card should be represented by the Hebrew letter *tet*, which signifies the serpent.

Although the Alliette (Etteilla) pack is not being considered here, it is worth noting that his Capucin, card number XVIII, is walking toward his left, as in the *minchiate*, and is accompanied by a dog. Alliette also gave this card the significance 'the Traitor', which, as we shall see, really belongs to card XII.

Pitois describes the traditional card, under the name of 'The Veiled Lamp': 'an old man who walks leaning on a stick and holding in front of him a lighted lantern half hidden by his cloak'.

Even Waite hardly changed the representation on this card: his hermit also has his hood up, however, and the light of the lantern is a hexagram star.

Interpretation. This card is concerned with time in all its aspects. Kronos, one of the oldest of the Greek gods, consumed each of his children as it was born; we may interpret this as a mythic representation of the way in which we all must succumb to Time:

'Time, like an ever-rolling stream
Bears all its sons away'

or of the attempts that we all make to stop the passage of time. The hourglass is a symbol of time, but it has an added significance in that it can be reversed at any moment. This is why Kronos, later known to the Romans as Saturn, is also related to Ouroboros, the serpent with the tail in his mouth. The hermit, who spends his life in solitary contemplation, is attempting to defeat time in his own way: its passing means nothing to him.

But this card is also concerned with the wisdom that time brings. The lantern that the hermit carries reminds us of the philosopher Diogenes, who had nothing but contempt for temporal power, and who carried a lantern in the dark, looking for one honest man.

In his negative aspects, the Hermit represents the tendency to escape from the responsibilities of everyday life: the holy man usually has every justification for withdrawing from the world around, but nevertheless his existence in his cell is in some ways a privileged and protected one, which he may exploit to his advantage. Knowledge and wisdom, too, may be misapplied; perhaps it was this aspect of the Hermit which caused Alliette to name this card the Traitor.

Another figure which has changed relatively little is the Hermit. In the Alliette and 'Spanish' pack (*far left*), however, card VIIII represents Justice. *Above*: 'The Veiled Lamp' of Pitois

X The Wheel of Fortune

(French: *la Roue de Fortune*   Italian: *Rota di Fortuna*   German: *das Glücksra*

This card bears one of the most powerful of medieval images, and lies appropriately at the heart of the Tarot pack. It has also undergone more distortion in the course of time than almost any other Tarot image, with the addition and removal of all sorts of significant images.

The turning wheel was used by medieval artists and thinkers to symbolise many different aspects of life: from the daily motion of the sun and planets to the cycle of punishment in hell. The traditional form of the wheel of fortune showed three figures on the wheel, and a fourth below it. Seated at the top was a crowned king, with the word *Regno* (I reign); ascending on the wheel was a young man with the word *Regnabo* (I shall reign); descending on the wheel was an older man with the word *Regnavi* (I have reigned). The figure below the wheel was an old man on hands and knees, with the words *sum sine regno* (I am without reign).

The 'Bembo' card of the Wheel of Fortune is very like this; blindfolded Fortune sits at the centre of the wheel, but the figure at the top of the wheel has become a cherub with ass's ears, The *minchiate* card is similar, but without the figure of Fortune: the man at the

top of the wheel, holding an orb in his hand, has a complete ass's head, and the descending figure has a rather devil-like head. The card in the 'Gringonneur' pack, which has rather remarkably been identified by all commentators as Fortune, is in fact The World, and will be described under that heading.

The 'traditional' Tarot card design takes these medieval tendencies a little further. The top of the wheel is occupied by a crowned monkey, holding a sword in his left paw, and with some kind of wings or high-shouldered cloak behind him. Another monkey, wearing a sort of striped skirt, descends on the wheel; while what could be either a monkey or a dog ascends. There is no fourth figure on the ground and, although the wheel has a cranked handle, there is nobody turning it.

This card in the Swiss pack is interesting in that it departs further from the traditional design than any other in this pack. Fortune's wheel stands on the edge of a cliff, and she herself, almost naked, is cranking it. Seated on the top of the wheel are a young couple in late eighteenth century dress: the man appears unconcerned, but the girl is looking apprehensively over her shoulder at the abyss beneath. Below her, a young man is just falling from the wheel. Interestingly, a rosebush blooms between the supports of the wheel.

Eliphas Lévi was responsible for the next development in the design of the Wheel of Fortune. In his *Key of the Mysteries* he reproduced a drawing of 'the tenth key of the Tarot': in this the crowned monkey has become unequivocally a winged sphinx, the ascending figure is a dog carrying the winged staff of Hermes, and the descending figure is a horned devil with a trident. These three figures are labelled respectively *Archée* ('made highest'), *Azoth* (a word invented by alchemists to describe a hypothetical first principle) and *Hyle* (the raw material of man, the substance of his purely animal nature). This design was followed by Oswald Wirth, but without the three labels; in addition, Wirth's wheel is supported in some kind of crescent-shaped boat, with the serpents of Asklepios twined about the support.

Pitois' description is clearly based on Lévi's ideas. The card is called 'The Sphinx': on the right side of the wheel Hermanubis 'the spirit of God', tries to climb the wheel, while on the left Typhon, the spirit of evil, is cast down. 'The Sphinx, balanced on top of the wheel, holds a sword in its lion's paw. It personifies Destiny ever ready to strike left or right . . .'

Waite's design moves even further away from the traditional. Derived from a drawing

The Wheel of Fortune has undergone extraordinary modifications, from the medieval image of the 'Bembo' pack (*right*) to the Egyptian exoticism of Pitois (*above*). Titian's 'Allegory of Prudence' (*below*) explains the identification of this card with Prudence

LA ROUE DE FORTUNE

10 LA ROVE DE FORTVNE

ROTA DI FORTUNA

ROTA DI FORTUNA

10 Diritto: LA SALUTE

10 Jod

LA TEMPLANZA

10 Rovescio: PRETE

PRVDENCIA XXXV

THE WHEEL OF FORTUNE

WHEEL of FORTUNE.

The significance of the Tarot trumps

Below: the Wheel of Fortune, from a fifteenth century manuscript in the Bodleian Library. This was a very common piece of popular imagery in the Middle Ages

in Lévi's *Sanctum Regnum*, the wheel is now a stylised circular shape, bearing the letters R-O-T-A, which can also be read as T-A-R-O, and between these the Hebrew letters *yod-he-vau-he*, the name of God. At the top of the wheel sits a sphinx, the jackal-headed figure of Anubis rises at the right, and a serpent descends at the left. The stylised spokes of the wheel are decorated with the alchemical symbols for mercury, sulphur, salt and water, and in the four corners of the card (echoing the traditional design of the card called The World) are the four mystical animals of Revelation: man, the eagle, the bull and the lion.

Interpretation. The cycles of the lunar month and the solar year, the cycle of generation and regeneration – 'birth, copulation and death' – the wheel of the sun itself, the wheels within wheels of fate, the circular transformation from one to another of the Aristotelian elements (earth, fire, air, water): all these meanings and many more are comprised in the symbols of this card.

The king with the ass's ears of the medieval image is Midas, who could turn everything into gold: in a musical contest between

Apollo and the satyr Marsyas, Midas voted for Marsyas, and in revenge Apollo gave him the ears, which he had to hide by wearing a Phrygian cap.

The later metamorphosis of the figures on the wheel may well be the incorporation of another piece of medieval imagery: one of the figures for the cardinal virtue of Prudence, which is otherwise missing from this pack. As Cicero, the Roman orator, put it in the first century BC: 'Prudence consists of . . . Memory, Intelligence and Foresight'. These three parts of Prudence were frequently represented by a three-headed figure with the heads of an elderly man or wolf, a mature man or lion, and a young man or dog, respectively.

This card, then, signifies change, and the ability to experience change prudently: knowing (to quote Cicero again) 'what is good, what is bad, and what is neither good nor bad'. And the card reminds us that few changes are permanent and irreversible; sooner or later an upward swing of fortune is followed by a fall, the wheels of destiny turn slowly but they always turn full circle in the end.

XI Fortitude or Strength

(French: *la Force*   Italian: *la Forza*   German: *die Kraft*)

The second of the classical virtues can be represented by a number of minor variations upon a single image. The 'Gringonneur' card shows a seated woman who is breaking a column in half, apparently using some sort of 'karate chop'. There are two rather different representations of Fortitude in the da Tortona and 'Bembo' cards: the former shows a woman holding the jaws of a snarling lion, and the latter is a picture of Hercules with his club subduing the Nemean lion. In the *minchiate* pack and the *tarocchi*, these images are combined as a woman, attended by a lion, snapping a pillar in two.

The traditional packs all follow the example of da Tortona; the only remarkable feature is the broad-brimmed hat worn by the woman, which is very similar in style to that worn by the Magician. The Swiss pack, however, chooses the image of Hercules – although he has laid down his club and is wrestling with the animal.

Oswald Wirth followed the traditional design without modification. Pitois, similarly, identified this card as 'The Tamed Lion': a young girl who with bare hands is closing, without effort, the jaws of a lion.

In fact, it is impossible to tell, in the design of any card described so far, whether the woman is closing, opening or merely holding the lion's jaws. Waite's design, however, makes it quite clear that Strength is closing the lion's jaws; although a garland of flowers, which appears to link the girl with the lion, nevertheless makes this a gesture of somewhat ambiguous significance.

Above: Pitois identified this card as 'The Tamed Lion'. The broken column of the 'Gringonneur' card also appears as an attribute of Fortitude in the *tarocchi*. Note that Waite's card is numbered VIII

XI

LA FORCE

11 LA FORCE

11 LA FORZA

LA FORZA

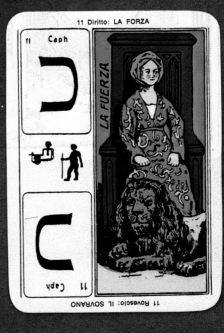

11 Diritto: LA FORZA

11 Caph

LA FUERZA

11 Caph

11 Rovescio: IL SOVRANO

FORTEZA · XXXVI

XI

FORCE

VIII

STRENGTH.

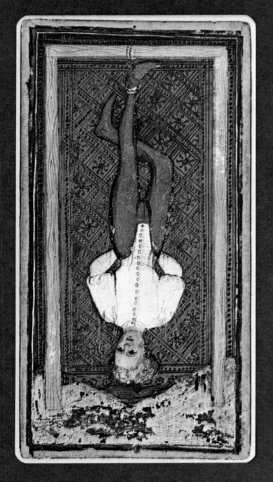

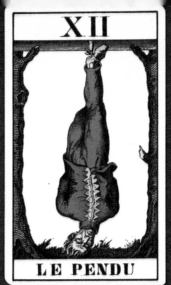

LE PENDU

12 | LE PEND

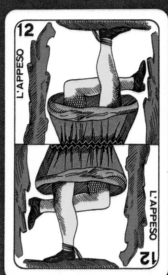

THE HANGED MAN

THE HANGED MAN.

Interpretation. The woman wrestling un-armed with the lion is Cyrene, nymph of the goddess Artemis (Diana). She was seen by Apollo who fell in love with her and carried her off in his chariot to Libya, where she gave birth to Aristaeus, who became the equivalent of the Thessalian god Pan.

The breaking of the pillar reminds us of another personification of strength, the Biblical hero Samson, who (although blind-ed) brought down the pillars of the temple. He was often represented as a Biblical equiv-alent of Hercules, holding a lion's jaws in exactly the way portrayed on this card. But the most evocative image for medieval man was of course that of Hercules himself, the archetypal hero of the Greeks. He spent twelve years under the orders of Eurystheus, the king of Greece, and performed twelve heroic labours, the first of which was killing the Nemean lion. While wearing the skin of this lion as a robe, Hercules was invincible.

This card, then signifies strength: strength of purpose, spiritual strength and moral courage, as well as sheer physical strength. Its message can be one of warning, meaning that bravery and resolve will be needed to meet a coming danger. And it can also suggest caution against abusing one's strength, using it to dominate others, whether physically or spiritually. The man who uses his intellectual superiority like a goad is as guilty of this as the man who bullies others by the strength of his arm.

XII The Hanged Man

(French: *le Pendu*   Italian: *l'Apesso*   German: *der Gehängte*)

No card in the Tarot pack has provoked more discussion than this one. Court de Gebelin, rightly realising that the pack lacked a card for Prudence, decided that this was it. 'You find it in its correct place between Fortitude and Temperance, a man hung by the heels. But why is he hung? This is the work of a presumptuous cardmaker who, misunderstanding the beauty of the allegory, has taken upon himself to correct it. . . . Prudence can only be represented in an intelligible manner as a standing man who, having put one foot forward, has lifted the other and now stands there examining the ground where he can place it safely. This card, then, is the man with his foot sus-pended, *pede suspenso*; but the ignorant cardmaker has made it a man suspended by his feet.'

For Court de Gebelin, in other words, the card is upside down, and it appears, as he described it, in an eighteenth century Belgian pack. The argument is very plausible, and it is fortunate that we have surviving cards from the oldest packs to show that it is wrong. For this card in the 'Gringonneur' pack is clearly of a young redheaded man who has been hung by one foot from the crossbar of a gibbet. This was the old punish-ment for debtors:

He by the heels him hung upon a tree
And baffl'd so, that all which passed by
The picture of his punishment might see

as Spenser put it in *The Faerie Queene*, some 400 years ago. In each hand the man holds a bag of coins that he has come by unlawfully. This is Judas, with the thirty pieces of silver he earned by betraying Christ; and, as the Bible says, he took a rope and hung himself. This is the card otherwise known as The Traitor.

In the 'Bembo' pack, the hanged man has his hands presumably tied behind his back, and his legs are crossed in a shape like the figure 4; this is the image that was adopted for all the 'traditional' cards. Even in the

Swiss pack it is substantially the same, although the crossing of the legs is not represented clearly, and the position of the arms is also rather vague.

Wirth's Hanged Man is very similar, but two bags of money can be seen, one beneath each armpit, with gold and silver coins falling from them. Pitois' description in-cludes an attempt to explain the graphic symbolism of the figure. He calls it 'The

From the earliest packs, the Hanged Man has been unequivocally hung by his feet; only a surviving eighteenth century Belgian pack antedates Court de Gebelin's insistence that this is a representation of a prudent man with one foot poised, printed upside down by mistake. Alliette and related packs, however, devote card XII to a representation of Prudence

Sacrifice': 'a man hung by one foot from a gallows which rests on two trees each of which has six branches cut from the trunk. The hands of this man are tied behind his back, and the bend of his arms forms the base of an inverted triangle the summit of which is his head. It is the sign of violent death encountered by tragic accident or in expiation of some crime, and accepted in a spirit of heroic devotion to Truth and Justice. The twelve lopped branches signify the extinction of life, the destruction of the twelve houses of the horoscope. The inverted triangle symbolises catastrophe.'

Only Waite's design is significantly different. Instead of a gibbet between two trees, the man hangs from a T-shaped cross. His legs are crossed in the 4-shape, and his arms are behind his back, but there is a bright halo about his head.

It is noticeable that there is no consistency in which foot the figure hangs by. On some cards he hangs by the left foot, on others by the right, and on at least one of the 'traditional' packs – the Swiss 1JJ pack published by Müller – he hangs by both.

Interpretation. In spite of the connection with Judas, and the gruesomeness of the idea of a hanged man, it is incorrect to regard this as a card of evil meaning; it is significant that, in nearly every representation, there is no look of discomfort on the man's face, despite his position.

Several commentators have drawn attention to the parallel with the words of Odin in The Lay of the High One:

Wounded I hung on a wind-swept gallows
For nine long nights.
Pierced by a spear, pledged to Odin,
Offered, myself to myself;
The wisest know not from whence spring
The roots of that ancient rood.

The tree was Yggdrasil, the World Tree, and Odin was the Norse god of the dead, but it would be unwise to pursue the parallel too closely. One-eyed Odin, with his eight-legged horse, who moved among the heroes as an old man in a wide-brimmed hat and cloak, is not the hanged man of the Tarot. Perhaps, however, the myth of Odin, initiated into the mysteries by nine nights of pain, is one form of a tradition that goes back into the mists of antiquity. For the idea of the man who is redeemed by suffering, and who by his suffering also redeems others, is far older than the stories of Odin, of Christ, of Mithra, or of any other god-like being. We remember, in particular, Attis, often represented as a handsome young man hung upon a tree.

The meaning of the Tarot is not always as it seems, and as we look at them the shapes shift and change. Judas the traitor, the symbol of faithlessness, becomes the initiate of the mysteries, the agent who sets the fore-ordained drama in motion: as we impose one personality upon him, he shifts easily into another. Odin was known as a shape-shifter, but the greatest of all was the 'Old Man of the Sea', Proteus. He could change his form at will: the important point was not to be frightened by the changes, when he would relent and give advice drawn from his knowledge of the events that were to come.

The card of the Hanged Man, then, may mean what you will. It symbolises adaptability and the desire to learn; it brings knowledge of the future and new understanding of the past; it means change – not the slow inevitable change of the Wheel of Fortune, but sudden violent change, demanding sacrifice. Yet it counsels you not to fear that change, but to face it bravely.

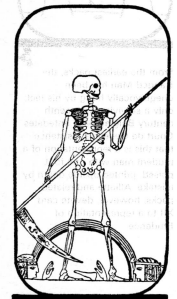

Although Death appears mounted on a horse in the 'Gringonneur' and da Tortona packs, he does not reappear in this form until the design of A. E. Waite (*bottom, far right*). The Spanish 'Great Patriarch' (*centre, far right*) is clearly derived from the traditional card VIII, the Lovers

XIII Death

(French: *la Mort*   Italian: *la Morte*   German: *der Tod*)

Here is another powerful symbol from medieval iconography, the image of Death as a skeleton mounted on a horse and carrying his scythe, trampling over the fallen bodies of kings, popes and cardinals. This is how he appears in the da Tortona and 'Gringonneur' packs, and in the *minchiate*. In the first two of these packs he has a white scarf bound round his head with the ends flying; this same feature is repeated in the 'Bembo' pack, but Death here is standing, with a strung bow in his hand. In another fifteenth century pack, by Cicognara, he stands with his scythe over his shoulder, leering in a cardinal's broad hat and cape: the words *son fine* (it is the end) emerge on a ribbon from his mouth.

Traditional packs are all very similar. Death, a naked skeleton, walks forward with his scythe in the reaping position, over a field in which heads, hands, feet and bones

are the main crop. In the Swiss pack the stance is identical, but the field is clear.

Oswald Wirth chose the same image as the traditional packs, and like them placed a crown upon one of the heads; there is no apparent additional feature in his design. Pitois also described this card without modification, giving it the name 'The Scythe' and interpreting it as the emblem of destruction and perpetual rebirth of all forms of Being in the domain of Time.

Waite's design, as might be expected, takes the elements from a number of different cards and combines them in an idiosyncratic way. Death is without a scythe, or a weapon of any kind, but he is dressed from head to foot in black armour. He rides a white horse and carries in his left hand a black banner with a white five-petalled heraldic rose. In the field through which he rides are a dead king, a child, a

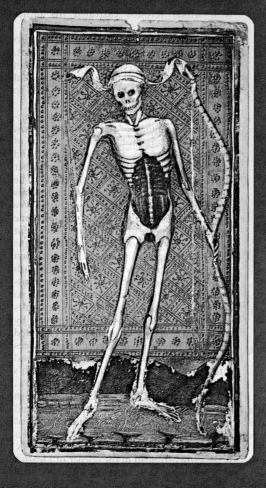

XIII

LA MORT

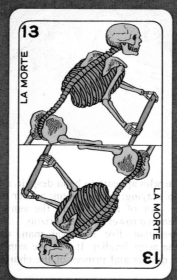

13

LA MORTE

LA MORTE

13

13 Diritto: MATRIMONIO - UNIONE

13 Mem

EL GRAN PATRIARCA

13 Rovescio: MATRIMONIO MANCATO

Mem 13

XIII

DEATH

XIII

DEATH.

for the wretched peasant: it was the only institution of democracy. The figure of Death was a warning of the vanity of worldly wealth and position. His scythe was the scythe of Saturn and of Time, the scythe with which Kronos castrated his father Uranus.

So, while Death takes away, he also restores: every conclusion is also a new start. The field that he reaps, with its human remains like a charnel house, is also the field where Jason sowed the dragon's teeth to grow as armed men.

Death, indeed, is the symbol of transformation. In many of the traditional Tarot packs, Death is not named for fear of bringing ill-luck by mentioning him; and it is no coincidence that this card is number thirteen; but, as with The Lovers or The Hanged Man, its true significance depends upon the context in which it is found. We have seen how the Wheel of Fortune represents change of a cyclic, recurrent kind, and how the Hanged Man means change through sacrifice and the sudden reversal of circumstances; the card of Death can also symbolise change, but of a transforming kind, the passage through ordeal to some sort of rebirth. All the mystery cults of antiquity initiated their members by some kind of ceremony in which they enacted death and rebirth; in certain cults the novices descended into Hades like Orpheus and afterward, like him, returned to the earth's surface. The myth of Orpheus tells how, when he returned from Hades, he was torn to pieces by the Thracian women; his head was thrown into the river Hebrus and carried to Lesbos, where it caught in the fissure of a rock and there remained, delivering oracles. Is the crowned head in the corner of Death's field perhaps this head of Orpheus, still uttering oracles?

Right: the 'Gringonneur' figure of Death, on a dark, rather than a pale, horse. *Below*: the 'Solar Spirit' of Pitois. *Far right*: the Spanish pack, like Alliette, is again out of order, attributing card XIV, rather than XV, to the Devil

woman who appears to be in despair, and a bishop praying; behind them, a river flows at the foot of a bluff, and the sun rises between two towers on the horizon.
Interpretation. For medieval man, death was the great leveller. It was the same for kings, queens and princes of the church as

XIV Temperance

(French: *Tempérance*   Italian: *la Temperanza*   German: *die Mässigkeit*)

Here is the fourth and last of the classical virtues, portrayed in a traditional medieval way. In every pack, from the 'Bembo' and 'Gringonneur' to those of Wirth and Waite, we find the same figure. A woman – generally standing, but in the 'Gringonneur' pack and the *minchiate* sitting – pours liquid from a jug held in one hand to another jug held in the other. In the early packs she is crowned like the other virtues, but in the traditional packs and those that follow she has wings like an angel.

To modern man, brought up to believe that 'temperance' means moderation in the use of alcohol, the figure seems to be pouring water into wine to dilute it; but to medieval man the significance was more likely that of division: halving the contents of one jug by pouring some into the other.

Pitois gave this card a very different

meaning – 'The Solar Spirit: Initiative'. He described it as the Spirit of the Sun pouring the vital sap of life from one urn into another, 'the symbol of the combinations which are ceaselessly produced in all parts of Nature'.

Even Waite's design for this card does not depart far from the traditional image. Temperance, pouring from one chalice to another, stands beside a pool with one foot in the water. Behind her a path leads to the mountains and the rising sun, and beside the pool are yellow irises.
Interpretation. The ancient Greeks represented Iris very much like the traditional figure of Temperance: she wore a long flowing tunic and flew on her errands with a pair of golden wings. When the gods returned to Olympus she waited on them, serving ambrosia and nectar. Her companion in these duties was Ganymede, the cup

XIIII

TEMPERANCE

14 LA TEMPERANCE

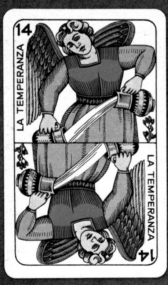

14 LA TEMPERANZA

LA TEMPERANZA 14

14 Diritto: FORZA MAGGIORE

14 Nun

EL DIABLO

14 Nun

14 Rovescio: FORZA MINORE

B· TEMPERANCIA XX XIIII B+

XIIII

TEMPERANCE

XIV

TEMPERANCE.

Above and right: medieval iconographers confused, deliberately or by accident, the figures of Ganymede (identified as the astrological Aquarius) and Iris, in their representation of Temperance

bearer; in primitive times he appears to have been thought of as the deity who sprinkled the earth with rain, and early astrologers identified him with Aquarius. It seems likely that medieval iconographers, either deliberately or by mistake, confused Iris with Ganymede.

No doubt they also infused this image with the significance of Christ's miracle of turning water into wine. The chalice of wine that changes into blood is a very powerful symbol in the celebration of the mass, and perhaps there is also a memory of the Eucharist as the second-century Gnostic Marcos celebrated it, with two chalices, one of water and one of wine, which he mixed together.

Few commentators have found very much to say about the significance of the card of Temperance: the image is a very simple one, and the concept behind it is equally simple. Temperance, of course, is not confined to alcohol; it means moderation in all things. Combined with this, too, is the concept of mercy; and the metal-worker who 'tempers' steel, bringing it exactly to the desired degree of hardness and elasticity, also knows the meaning of the word. Indeed, to keep one's temper, to be temperate in action and opinion, to keep a room, or an oven, at an even temperature – all these uses come from the same source. The card Temperance, appearing with other cards, will modify their significance, and always for the better.

XV The Devil

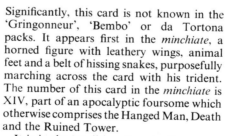

(French: *le Diable*   Italian: *il Diavolo*   German: *der Teufel*)

Significantly, this card is not known in the 'Gringonneur', 'Bembo' or da Tortona packs. It appears first in the *minchiate*, a horned figure with leathery wings, animal feet and a belt of hissing snakes, purposefully marching across the card with his trident. The number of this card in the *minchiate* is XIV, part of an apocalyptic foursome which otherwise comprises the Hanged Man, Death and the Ruined Tower.

It is in the 'traditional' packs that a new element emerges. The winged figure stands on some kind of a pedestal, holding in his left hand something that might be a sceptre or a sword but which, in some designs, bears an unexpected resemblance to the object (torch, key or piece of the mystery plant *haoma*) held in the left hand of so many statues from temples of the Roman god Mithra. Two lesser devils stand each side, fastened by a cord about the neck to a ring in the front of the pedestal. In certain packs, none of the figures has the usual short, goat-like horns, but rather a helmet from which sprout antlers; and the central figure wears a kind of breastplate with exaggerated breasts and sometimes an animal-like face at his belly.

The Swiss pack, however, returns to the

Eliphas Lévi's Goat of Mendes was supposed by him to be the idol worshipped by the Knights Templar. Its appearance contributed significantly to Oswald Wirth's design for the card of the Devil. The Spanish pack (*far right*) gives card XV to a figure that is obviously the Magician

medieval image: the devil has short horns, a curly tail concealing his nakedness, and cloven hoofs. He carries a pitchfork, and a woman sits despairingly at his feet, her head in her hands. The eighteenth century Belgian Tarot pack also has a devil of medieval derivation.

Wirth's design once more shows the influence of Eliphas Lévi. The Devil has become Lévi's invention, the 'Goat of Mendes', which he supposed to have been the idol worshipped by the Knights Templar. This has wide curling horns and a bearded face like a mountain goat, above a naked body with a woman's breasts, legs covered in green scales, hairy calves and cloven hoofs. The two minor devils are of fairly orthodox form, and are fastened to the central ring by what is called a 'cable-tow' in freemasonry. But among the symbolic additions to this card are the glyph which covers the goat's genitals – a combination of the sign for Mercury and the *crux ansata* – and the lettering of the words 'solve' and 'coagula' on the right and left arms respectively. 'Solve et coagula' ('Liquefy and solidify' is the closest translation) was the basic principle of medieval alchemy. As always with Lévi's modifications there is

LE DIABLE.

15 LE DIABLE

Above: the frightful, the terrible Typhon, 'who rises out of a flaming abyss and brandishes a torch above the heads of two men chained at his feet', as Pitois described it

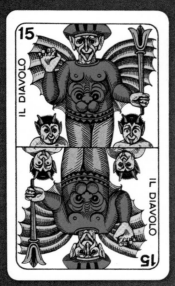

15 IL DIAVOLO

15 Diritto: MALINCONIA

15 Sameck

EL FALSO ADIVINO

15 Sameck

15 Rovescio: INDISPOSIZIONE

XV

THE DEVIL

XV

THE DEVIL .

47

little or no justification for these changes and additions to the Tarot figure.

By comparison, Waite's design is positively conventional, but it contrives deliberately to reflect the design of his card for The Lovers. The pose of the bat-winged Devil is similar to that of the angel, and the two captive devils are a man and a woman. The Devil's right hand is raised in a strange gesture, the first and second, and third and fourth, fingers together, with the glyph of Saturn on the palm; and his left holds an inverted torch.

Interpretation. Medieval people knew very well who the Devil was: they recognised his angelic origin, but they gave him features derived from all the non-Christian gods whom they saw as threats to their religion.

First of all this is 'the frightful, the terrible Typhon', the monstrous offspring of Hera, the same creature as Set, the evil brother of Osiris. 'All that is creation and blessing comes from Osiris; all that is destruction and

perversity arises from Set.' The Egyptians represented Set with a forked tail and two stiff square-cut ears; later these ears became horns.

But the helmet with antler-like horns from the traditional Tarot is the helmet of Kernunnos, the Celtic god of pre-Roman times. And the goat horns and feet are those of the Greek god Pan, who finally came to represent the universal god, the Great All.

Above all, however, as has already been indicated above, the Devil of the Tarot incorporates many features derived from the religion of Mithraism, which flourished at the time when Christianity was first struggling to establish itself. Mithra was one of the most ancient of gods: he appears in the earliest Indian texts, the Vedas, and was well-established before 1400 BC. He appears as an important god in Zoroastrianism, where his adversary is Ahriman, the representative of Zervan, whom the Romans called Saturn.

In Mithraism, Zervan was represented in various similar ways. He usually had wings and the head of a lion, and carried a pair of keys; sometimes he had claw-like or cloven feet, and a serpent twined about his body like the tail of Set; sometimes the lion head was featured on his belly. Mithra himself was generally represented standing between two smaller figures, one carrying a torch the right way up, the other carrying it inverted.

We can see, then, that this card symbolises above all the power of the adversary: if plans are being made, it represents the way in which circumstances seem to conspire against the realisation of those plans; and it represents the darker, subconscious side of human nature, which often causes us to act against our best interests. It can mean an enemy; but it can also mean a friend whose personality is so strong that he can influence our decisions, for good as well as bad. Whenever the card of the Devil appears, it signals caution: plans should be looked at with care, decisions reconsidered.

Above: the Mithraic figure of Zervan, with attendant torch-bearers (dadophori), discovered in a mithraeum in Ostia. *Right*: the horned figure of Set (*left*) leads two attendant figures by ropes, exactly as on the Devil card

XVI The Tower

(French: *la Maison de Dieu*   Italian: *la Torre*   German: *das Haus Gottes*)

A tower, struck by lightning. In the traditional packs the tower has a crown-like castellated top which has been tilted sideways by the bolt of lightning; bricks and tongues of flame are falling on both sides, and two male figures are tumbling to the ground. In the 'Gringonneur' pack these figures are absent, and the top of the tower is undisturbed, but stones and flickers of flame are falling on the right-hand side. The card does not appear in the surviving 'Bembo' pack, nor in the da Tortona pack, where the World card has been wrongly identified as the Tower; in *minchiate* packs a naked woman, presumably Eve, is emerging from a

doorway in the tower, closely followed by a man, while fire falls from heaven.

Oswald Wirth's version is substantially the same as the traditional; one of the falling figures wears a small crown, and the lightning flash comes from a sun partially visible in the top right corner. This also is how Pitois described it.

In the Waite design, the crown-like top of the tower has become a real crown, which has been blasted off, but otherwise it remains substantially the same as the traditional Tarot cards.

Interpretation. This is yet another card of the Tarot which combines a very considerable

Above: In spite of its Egyptian style of design, the Pitois card is very similar to the traditional cards. The Spanish pack (*left*) devotes card XVI to the Last Judgment

The significance of the Tarot trumps

Right: a representation of the falling tower from the Golden Legend, in Reims cathedral; and the figureless Ruined Tower of the 'Gringonneur' pack.
Far right: with characteristic perverseness, the Alliette and related packs make card XVII Death

number of strong medieval images. The most obvious is a story from the Golden Legend which tells how, when the Holy Family fled from Herod, their entry into each town caused the pagan temples and altars to tumble. Representations of this story appear in carvings in several medieval cathedrals.

Next to this, we must consider a combination of the story of Pentecost, in which the descent of tongues of flames from heaven caused the disciples to speak in different languages, with the story of the Tower of Babel, whose builders were made to speak, each with a different language, as punishment for their presumption in building a tower up to heaven. The *minchiate* representation is clearly connected with the expulsion of Adam and Eve from the Garden of Eden, and there are also echoes of the story of the destruction of Sodom.

The true medieval meaning of Maison de Dieu (or, more commonly, Maison-Dieu) is 'hospital', but it seems more likely that 'House of God' is intended, and that the reference is either to the Golden Legend, or to the striking of the temple in Jerusalem by lightning at the time of the crucifixion.

The meaning of the card is punishment: for presumptuous pride, for the pursuit of forbidden knowledge, or for actual transgression of the moral code. It can also stand for pride itself, for male sexuality, or for the finger of God raised in warning. In certain contexts it may represent the gift, or the confusion, of foreign tongues; and finally it can symbolise the burning flame of divine inspiration, which must be received with humility lest it should destroy.

XVII The Stars

(French: *l'Étoile*   Italian: *le Stelle*   German: *die Gestirne*)

The usual English name of this card is 'the Star', but its Italian and German names show it for what it really represents: the whole of the celestial sphere.

Medieval philosophers imagined the planets turning about the earth in a succession of seven spheres; outside these turned the celestial sphere, and beyond this the *primum mobile*, the 'prime mover', and the *prima causa*, or First Cause. All these are represented in the 'Mantegna' *tarocchi*, but only the signs of the zodiac and the Sun, Moon and stars are included in the *minchiate*.

The *minchiate* card justifies the use of the title 'the Star', for it clearly shows one of the magi, following the star that hung over the

stable at Bethlehem, and bearing his precious gift in his right hand.

The early Tarots, in contrast, all show a crowned female figure, facing right and holding up a single eight-pointed star. In the 'Bembo' pack the star is in her left hand; in one of the surviving cards by Cicognara, the star is in her right hand, and she holds a hooded falcon on her left wrist.

The traditional packs introduce an entirely new element: a naked, or near-naked, woman, who kneels on the shore with two pitchers, emptying one or both into the water. Above her the sky is full of stars: sometimes seven and sometimes eight, generally with one much bigger than the rest.

L'ÉTOILE

XVII.

17 LES ETOILES ⊐

17 LE STELLE

17 Diritto: MORTALITA'

17 Pe

LA MUERTE

17 Rovescio: ROVINA

B· SPERANZA·XXXVIIII· 39

XVII

THE STAR

XVII

THE STAR.

The significance of the Tarot trumps

Below: the Star of Hope, as Pitois described it

Right: the development of the Tarot card of the Moon shows the combination of various concepts associated with the moon, such as the hounds of Diana and the astrological sign of Cancer. But card XVIII in the Spanish and Alliette packs is the Hermit

Often there is a tree in the distance, with a bird perched on its summit.

The Wirth design is very similar, but the eight stars are of varying sizes, and the tree has been replaced by a bush with a single rose, with a butterfly on it. Pitois identifies the figure as that of Hope 'which scatters its dew upon our saddest days; she is naked in order to signify that Hope remains with us when we have been bereft of everything'.

In Waite's design, the naked woman empties one pitcher into a pool, and the other upon dry land; the bird perching on the distant tree is an ibis.

Interpretation. Who is the naked woman? Is she Hope, as Pitois and others have suggested? Certainly, in the da Tortona pack and the *minchiate*, Hope is portrayed as a crowned woman, her hands joined in prayer, but with her gaze fixed upon a ray of light, in a pose very similar to that of the figure in the 'Bembo' and Cicognara designs.

Further investigation suggests that she is of far more ancient lineage. The Persians, whose priests were the magi, worshipped Mithra together with the goddess of the waters, Anahita, who was also identified with the planet Venus. The Sumerians in their turn connected Venus with Inanna, who eventually became Aphrodite of the Greeks, born from the wave of the sea and carried naked to the shore. In the 'Mantegna' pack,

Venus bathes naked in a pool, pouring water on herself from a pitcher; and the bird which appears on so many of the Tarot cards turns out to be a dove, the most well-known of the symbols associated with Venus.

In this card Venus, or Aphrodite, is taken as the symbol of all the planets and stars beyond the sun and moon; she is the goddess of the waters of rebirth flowing from 'behind the region of the summer stars'; she is the source of the dew that falls from heaven just before the dawn.

The bird perched on the tree may be a dove or a hawk; both represent the soul. Or we may remember the dove and the raven that Noah released from the ark.

The significance of this card is, first of all, rebirth and new beginning. The morning star signals the arrival of Aphrodite to awaken Adonis; the pitchers emptied into the pool remind us of the bath of rejuvenation, and of the fountain that stood at the heart of Paradise and fed the rivers of the world; the dove, or raven, represents the re-emergence of Earth from the waters after the Deluge.

The presence of the goddess known as Anahita, Inanna, Aphrodite or Venus also promises pleasure, and we recall the rich gifts brought by the magi to Bethlehem. Above all, the distant stars symbolise hope and the promise of salvation.

XVIII The Moon

(French: *la Lune*   Italian: *la Luna*   German: *der Mond*)

This is another medieval image that we can see gradually changing from one thing into another. In the 'Gringonneur' pack the image is the simplest: two astrologers are observing the crescent moon, measuring her orb with dividers, and making calculations in a book. A second element enters in the 'Bembo' pack: here the goddess Diana stands with the crescent moon in her right hand, and a broken bow in her left. The usual *minchiate* design is similar to the 'Gringonneur' except that there may be only one astrologer; but there is another *minchiate* design which represents Diana, the crescent on her head, striding along with one of her hounds.

It is from these disparate elements that the traditional Tarot card has evolved. This shows the moon shining full in the sky; the two astrologers are replaced by two of Diana's hounds, baying at the moon; and from the waters below (for the moon rules over the waters) crawls a crayfish-like animal which is in fact the zodiacal sign for Cancer, the 'house' of the moon. At each side of the landscape behind the baying hounds can be seen a squat tower.

In the Swiss pack, this design has undergone the same kind of dissociation as the Chariot in the same pack. The card is effectively divided in two: in the upper half

the crescent moon shines while a young man, his dog beside him, serenades a girl on a balcony; and in the lower half Cancer, flanked by two shapes looking like primitive shellfish, stands against a wall in which two blank-looking doors are half visible to left and right.

The Wirth design once again follows the traditional design fairly closely: the crustacean is a little more crab-like in its form, and one of the dogs is white while the other has been turned into a dark grey wolf. Pitois calls this card 'Deceptions'. The Waite card, also, is similar; it also has a dog and a wolf.

Interpretation. The moon, which changes its form so rapidly, and which can be found each night in a different part of the sky, has long been the symbol of fickleness. Its apparent connection with the menstrual cycle (indeed, the word 'menstruum' as well as 'month' may well have come from the same root as 'moon') has made the moon representative of all that is changeable in women. The huntress goddess Artemis, the Roman Diana, was renowned for the way in which she turned vindictively on those who fell in love with her, or who tried to take advantage of her femininity.

Ancient astronomers – not, of course, those of inland Asia or the Mediteranean countries – soon discovered the connection

LA LUNE

18 LA LVNE

18 LA LUNA

LA LUNA

18 Diritto: L'EREMITA

18 Tsade

EL ERMITAÑO

18 Rovescio: TRADIMENTO - FELLONIA

LVNA XXXXI

XVIII

THE MOON

THE MOON.

of the moon with the tides, and in medieval astrology she was believed to control all activities connected with water. Many engravings, illuminations and wood-cuts illustrate this connection, representing the moon in her chariot above scenes of boating and fishing, watermills at work and ships setting sail. And there is almost invariably one other activity which links the moon with another card of the Tarot pack: in one corner a travelling mountebank will be found, performing the cup-and-balls trick exactly like the Magician of card I.

Perhaps because, in earlier days, all women were thought to have weaker minds than men; perhaps because the moon was believed to exert its tidal influence on the liquids of the body, and particularly the brain – but it was long believed that the moon was associated with madness, making men and women 'lunatics'. Legends abound of those who were driven insane by sleeping in the light of the full moon, and nightmares and weird dreams were also associated with her influence. Witches rode abroad in the light of the moon, changing their shape, and bringing misfortune to those on whom they cast their spells.

This card is the symbol of uncertainty, of changeability. It warns us that we should not put our full trust in appearances, that even those things and people that we put most reliance upon may unaccountably let us down. The dogs who howl at the moon are pursuing an unattainable ideal.

Far left: In this woodcut from *Die Wirkungen der Planeten* (1470), the Magician is seen plying his trade under the influence of the Moon. Note the very strange position of his feet. *Left*: the design of the 'Gringonneur' card incorporates the two astrologers who were subsequently transmogrified into hounds. *Above*: the Pitois version of the Moon. *Below*: the Pitois version of the Sun

XIX The Sun

(French: *le Soleil*   Italian: *il Sole*   German: *die Sonne*)

The sun in splendour, his full face pouring down heat upon the earth, while on the ground below two children stand together in front of a low wall: this is the traditional design for this card, exemplified in a variety of different packs.

But it did not begin quite in this way. The 'Gringonneur' design is of a young fair-haired woman, walking alone with a distaff in her hand, spinning thread; above her the full sun shines down, and the origin of the wall may perhaps be seen in the incised gold background which represents the earth behind her. The 'Bembo' pack shows a cherub, carrying the sun on high as a shining face. The 'Mantegna' *tarocchi* represent the sun-god Helios driving his quadriga drawn by white horses across the sky, with the young Icarus falling to earth below; oddly, and without explanation, a scorpion (reminiscent of the crayfish on the Moon card, but not astrologically associated with the Sun) floats in the sky above.

In the *minchiate* pack, the Sun shines down upon a pair of seated lovers; and the Swiss pack, which often shows many deviations from tradition, is almost identical in its design.

The Wirth design is only a slight modification of the traditional form: the two figures are a young man and woman, standing in a flowery circle. Pitois identifies the subject as 'The Blazing Light: Earthly Happiness'. The Waite design, however, is significantly different: a single naked child, carrying a huge banner on a staff, rides the back of a white horse, while behind him the sun shines into a walled garden which is crowded with sunflowers.

Interpretation. Many commentators have identified this card with the god Apollo but, although Apollo was closely connected with the Sun, he was never represented in this form. If we take this to be Helios, then the two children may be his two sons by Perse, Aeetes and Perses; or his two daughters Circe and Pasiphae; or his children by Naera, Phaetusa and Lampetia, the guardians of his flocks. Perhaps they are the boy Aeetes and the girl Circe, who lived together on the island of Aeaea, where Circe was the goddess of love. She is best remembered for the enchantments by which she turned all the companions of Odysseus into swine when they landed on her island.

On the other hand, the appearance of these

XVIIII

LE SOLEIL

19 LE SOLEIL

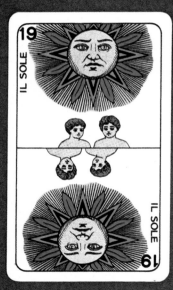

19 IL SOLE

IL SOLE 19

19 Diritto: CATASTROFE

19 Coph

LA DESTRUCCION DEL TEMPLO

19 Rovescio: PRIGIONE

A   SOL XXXXIIII   44

XVIIII

THE SUN

THE SUN .

by making flames flicker above their heads.

The Sun has always been of the greatest importance to mankind: it is the source of all life, warming and nourishing animals and plants, and its disappearance at night, or during an eclipse, fills primitive man with fear. Above the tropics, the gradual strengthening of the Sun in spring, and its weakening in autumn, were occasions of great religious festivals. Apollo, who represented the Sun, became a god of many different functions. He made the crops ripen, and protected them from pests; he killed from a distance, but he also healed sickness; he was also so pre-eminent among the lesser gods that he became the god of prophecy and divination for certain communities.

It is when we go further back, to the Babylonian god who came before Apollo, that we find a possible explanation for the scorpion in the 'Mantegna' card. The sun-god of the Babylonians was Shamash, who rode in his chariot each day across the sky, and returned each night to his home in the mountains of the East. Every morning, the doors of the mountain were opened, to let out the chariot, by the scorpion men who defended them.

Primarily, this card symbolises splendour and triumph, health and wealth, everything good that the Sun brings. The two young people below, whether they are children or lovers, are joined in friendship or affection. But we must remember that solitary figure with the distaff, in the 'Gringonneur' card. Is this Clotho, who spins the thread of every human life? And is one of the two children really the enchantress Circe? Beware the deceptions that are practised in the full light of day, 'the destruction that wasteth at noonday', and remember that the scorpion, who waits motionless in the sunlight, is also a symbol not only of treachery but of the possibility of self-destruction.

The design of the Sun is subject to more variations than almost any other card. From solitary woman spinner to cherub, from the Gemini to a pair of lovers and so full circle back to a naked infant on a white horse, the figures on this card have added a wide variety of meanings to its interpretation. *Above*: the astrological sign of Gemini. The 'Destruction of the Temple' (*left*) is assigned to this card in the Spanish pack

two children in the traditional design may be yet another example of confusion in copying this card from one cardmaker to another. In the 'Bembo' pack the World is held aloft by two cherubs, very similar to the one who holds aloft the Sun; alternatively, these may be the Dioscuri, or Gemini, from the *minchiate* pack. During the voyage of the *Argo*, Zeus showed his favour for these two

XX The Judgment

(French: *le Jugement*   Italian: *l'Angelo*   German: *das Weltgericht*)

The concept of the Last Judgment is one that extends through many different religions, but all the Tarot representations are concerned almost entirely with its Christian significance.

The traditional card shows an angel, the Archangel Michael, armed with a trumpet and leaning down from a cloud in a blaze of light. The trumpet bears a banner with a cross on it. A number of naked figures, generally three, are rising from the grave below. The Swiss card is very similar, but there are four figures, and the angel is very much less impressive and has no banner on his trumpet.

The image is substantially the same in the very earliest Tarots: in the 'Gringonneur' and da Tortona pack two angels lean out of a cloud; in the 'Bembo' card, God himself

is seen in heaven. The subject is absent from the *tarocchi*, which are concerned solely with human knowledge, and in the *minchiate* there is some doubt as to whether the angel flying over a town and sounding two trumpets is really the herald of the resurrection. The words 'Fama Vola' (Reputation flies) which appear on the card have caused it to be known as 'the Fame'.

Oswald Wirth's design bears a close resemblance to the traditional one. The cross on the angel's flag is slightly more complex, and he bears on his head a strange red cap fronted with a gold disc, but most of the graphic elements – the cloud and the light rays coming from it, the position and sex of the three resurrected figures – are disposed in exactly the same way. Pitois described this card as 'The Awakening of the Dead:

LE JUGEMENT

20 LE JVGEMENT

20 Diritto: FORTUNA - DIGNITA'

LA RUEDA DE LA FORTUNA

20 Resch

20 Resch

20 Rovescio: ELEVATEZZA

JUDGEMENT

JUDGEMENT.

Renewal'. 'A Spirit is blowing a trumpet over a half-open tomb. A man, a woman and a child, a collective symbol of the human trinity, are shown rising from this tomb. It is a sign of the change which is the end of all things, of Good as well as of Evil.'

Waite's design also is very little changed from the traditional. There are more resurrected figures in the distance, and each of the dead is risen from his or her own tomb, which 'float on the waters of emotion'.

Interpretation. Medieval man believed without question in the Last Judgment. Many religions teach that there is judgment of the dead; the concept of the Final Assize of the Dead comes partly from Judaism and partly from Zoroastrianism, and is about 2500 years old. Christianity shares with the latter religion the idea that there is both a judgment of the individual immediately after death, and a mass judgment of all humanity at the Last Trump.

This card signifies punishment or reward; it reminds us that we must be called to account for all that we have done, all that we have left undone, all that we have thought or planned. Rewards are few, while the penalties for failure are many, but we must remember that we learn through suffering. Through pain and disappointment we rise to final achievement.

The card of the Last Judgment is linked with the card of Death; through change and transformation we shall reach the ultimate reckoning.

The design of the Last Judgment has changed very little over the centuries. The so-called 'Wheel of Fortune' in the Alliette-type packs is clearly derived from the traditional design for the World (see following pages). *Below* the Last Judgment, from the cathedral of St-Lazare at Autun. Christ sits in majesty within a mandorla, the holy shape which reappears in the design of the World

XXI The World

(French: *le Monde*   Italian: *il Mondo*   German: *die Welt*)

Below: Pitois' Crown of the Magi: 'the sign with which the Magus decorates himself when he has reached the highest degree of initiation'. *Below right*: this card from the 'Gringonneur' pack has consistently been wrongly identified as Fortune. *Far right*: the 'Spanish' card of the Tyrant may represent Scipio Africanus the younger, the 'scourge of Carthage', who was granted a Roman triumph, and it clearly has close affinities with the Chariot

This is another example of what began as a relatively simple medieval image, and gradually accrued all sorts of significant additional elements. In the 'Bembo' pack, this card shows two winged cherubs, holding up a globe which contains a vast castle, standing on a rocky island surrounded by water, while overhead the stars blaze in the sky. In one of the da Tortona cards from the Visconti family collection a half-length figure of a woman, with a trumpet in her right hand and a wreath in her left, presides above a grand arch; below, there is a complete landscape, with ships on the sea, sailors in a river boat, mounted soldiers and a fisherman, hills, towers, castles, streams, fields, houses and meadows. By comparison, the 'Gringonneur' card is almost crude: a female figure with sceptre and orb stands on a globe which portrays walled towns on a succession of little hills. This globe is surrounded by a green sphere of air, and floats among stylised blue waves. It is this card that has been wrongly identified for over a century as 'Fortune'.

The World does not figure in the *tarocchi*, but the figure of Jupiter in this pack clearly contributes something to the development of the traditional image. Jupiter sits in an almond-shaped framework, holding an arrow to represent one of his thunderbolts in his right hand. On the top of the framework perches an eagle, a girl sits in the lower part, and wounded soldiers lie about.

The next stage in development occurs in the *minchiate*. Here, as in the 'Gringonneur' card, a female – but naked now, and with wings – stands on a globe ringed about with a sphere of air. She holds an arrow in her right hand, and a crown in her left; at equal distances round the globe are four winged heads to represent the four winds.

So we come to the traditional design for this card. A naked female figure, her left leg raised in the strange figure 4 shape we have already seen in the Emperor and the Hanged Man, and holding in either hand a rod like that held by the Magician, stands inside an almond-shaped wreath. At the four corners of the card are a winged man, an eagle, a bull and a lion. The Swiss design is similar, but the naked girl stands on both feet, and holds nothing in her hands but a narrow drapery (floating freely over the figure's shoulder in the traditional design); the wreath is more open and nearly circular and, while the bull and the lion appear in the lower corners, only the eagle appears above, flanked on either side by a bird of indeterminate species.

Wirth's card shows a complete re-working of the traditional design elements. The wreath is completely circular, and the figure appears to be running to the right, carrying both rods in her left hand. The four 'Beasts' are still in the corners, but their character has somehow been lost in the re-drawing. Pitois identifies this card as the Crown of the Magi ('The Reward') and describes it as a garland of roses surrounding a star; at equal distances around the garland are the four heads. Surprisingly, allowing for the differences in style, the Waite card is almost identical with the traditional one.

Interpretation. Let us look first at the significance of the four heads in the four corners of the card. It is easiest to tabulate their significance in medieval iconography:

Bull	Luke	earth
Lion	Mark	fire
Man	Matthew	water
Eagle	John	air

These four also came to stand for the four corners of the earth, or the four directions from which the winds blew; so we have the well-known night spell 'Matthew, Mark, Luke and John, Bless the bed that I lie on'. Paul Huson, in *The Devil's Picture Book*, compares this with the cabalist's

Before me Uriel, Behind me Raphael
At my right Michael, At my left Gabriel

XXI

LE MONDE

21 LE MONDE

21 IL MONDO

21 Diritto: TIRANNIA

21 Schin

ODIO AFRICANO — EL DÉSPOTA

21 Schin

21 Rovescio: TEMERITA'

B COSMICO·XXXIII

XXI

THE WORLD

XXI

THE WORLD.

and refers this further back to the ancient Babylonian spell:

Shamash before me, Sin behind me
Nergal at my right, Ningirsu at my left

Particularly interesting is the fact that the symbols of these four ancient gods are: for Sin an old man, for Ningirsu an eagle, for Nergal a lion, and for Shamash (in his form as Adad, god of prophecy) a bull.

There is no suggestion that this indicates a more ancient ancestry for the Tarot; but it is evidence of how old imagery of this sort can be, and how it can be passed on from generation to generation, becoming modified to fit the beliefs of the time.

The four beasts also remind us once again of the vision of Ezekiel; perhaps the figure within the wreath is a distorted image of the angelic visitor in the fiery wheel. But it is also the *spiritus mundi*, and, if we think of the four beasts as representing the four elements of Aristotle, it is the fifth, *aether*, or the philosopher's stone of the alchemists.

The almond shape of the wreath is the mandorla, one of the holiest of haloes, and the figure also has a close resemblance to medieval portrayals of Christ at the resurrection. A carving in Chartres Cathedral shows Christ in a mandorla, surrounded by the four beasts.

With the twenty-first card of the Tarot we have come full circle. The number 21 is itself magic: it is the sum of the first six numbers, and it is the product of 3×7, two numbers of great magical significance, while the sum of its component figures is also 3.

This card, therefore, means fulfilment, completion, arrival at a goal; yet, in spite of the holy and magical images that it incorporates, it is essentially a material world that we see here, the material world with which the spiritual world interpenetrates. It may indicate the end of one cycle of life, but we begin again on the cycle above, knowing that we have not yet attained release from the body.

The Fool

(French: *le Mat*   Italian: *il Matto*   German: *der Narr*)

And so we come to the central enigma of the Tarot Pack: the un-numbered Fool. But there is no doubt that he belongs here, for this card appears in the earliest Tarots. In the 'Gringonneur' pack he is a giant figure, more than 4 metres tall, clad in a yellow and red cap with ears, fool's motley and a loincloth. Between his hands he holds a string of fourteen gold discs, or beads, or perhaps brass bells; and four young men play about his feet. In the 'Bembo' pack he is ragged, with straw or feathers in his hair.

In the *minchiate* he is also a giant figure, or perhaps an adult among children; he is dressed in traditional fool's costume, with cap and bells and a toy sceptre, and he is playing with two figures who come a little above his waist. Two other designs contributed to the next stage in the development of this card. Firstly, there is the *minchiate* card of Diana (described above with the Moon); she is walking very much in the way of the Fool in the traditional pack, and one of her hounds walks behind her on a leash. Secondly, there is the Beggar card of the first series in the *tarocchi*: this shows a large and near-naked man, leaning upon a staff while dogs bark and prance at his heels.

The traditional card, then, shows us a bearded man dressed in motley with bells about his neck. With his left hand he is carrying over his right shoulder the typical tramp's stick with belongings tied in a cloth; in his right hand he holds a walking staff. The graphic quality of the design is very strong, and owes nothing to the cards that antedate it.

Behind the Fool prances a dog, and in some designs he appears to be tearing a hole in the Fool's breeches. Much has been read into this by commentators, but we must beware. A common item of dress for several hundred years was single hose, held up by strings known as 'points'; and it was quite common for the points to break, letting the hose hang down and exposing the naked flesh beneath. Other designs show the dog, sometimes so badly drawn that it looks more like a cat, actually biting the Fool's leg. We recall the nursery rhyme lines (a description of the first appearance of wandering gypsy bands in Europe):

Hark, hark, the dogs do bark
The beggars are coming to town;
Some in rags and some in bags
And some in velvet gown.

In the Swiss pack, the Fool looks very much like a *commedia dell'arte* character, in his particoloured suit, with bells on his cap and at his knees. He has no dog or belongings, and his staff is replaced by a short baton.

In Oswald Wirth's design the animal is undeniably a cat, or some other fierce feline. The Fool is clearly wearing single hose, and both have fallen down; he is dressed in motley, but without bells. Between his feet a flower droops; this is the same flower that Wirth included on several other cards — upright between the feet of the Magician, opening at the feet of the Emperor, and in full bloom in The Stars.

At some point in the seventeenth or eighteenth century, another element entered the design of this card. It probably came from Belgium, where packs of the early eighteenth century reveal a number of significant deviations in design; and it shows the Fool walking unaware toward the open jaws of a crocodile. In the Wirth card the crocodile is scarcely visible as a pair of

Right: the development of the Fool over the centuries clearly shows his relationship to two cards from the *tarocchi*, the Beggar (*near right*) and Mercury (*above*). As Mercury is also related to the Magician this happily completes the circle of the Major Arcana

MERCVRIO XXXXII

LE MAT.

LE FOV

IL MATTO

IL MATTO

78 Than

LA LOCURA
ó EL

ALQUI-
MISTA

78 Than

MISERO

THE FOOL

THE FOOL.

The significance of the Tarot trumps

Above: the Crocodile of Pitois.
Right: the giant Fool of the 'Gringonneur' pack resembles the huge figures paraded in numerous Lent carnivals

green jaws appearing over a distant beam of wood, but Pitois seized on this with enthusiasm, describing this card as 'The Crocodile: Expiation'. The Fool, he says, is 'a blind man carrying a full beggar's wallet about to collide with a broken obelisk, on which a crocodile is waiting with open jaws'.

Rather surprisingly, Waite did not incorporate this animal in his design. His Fool, a handsome young man with a rose in his left hand and his eyes on the sky, is about to step over a precipice; he is dressed in brightly decorated clothes, and carries a wallet on a stick over his right shoulder. The dog prances joyously beside him, and behind him the sun rises high in the sky.

Interpretation. The first point to be discussed is the meaning of the name *le mat* or *il matto*. Because the card is so named, and because it portrays a fool, this name has come to mean 'fool', but its derivation is very far from this. This is exactly the same word that appears in the Spanish 'matador', or in the word 'checkmate' in chess. It comes from a very old Persian word meaning 'to kill', or 'to put an end to'.

Do not suppose, however, that the Fool is death or an agent of death. He is not a messenger, nor an actor with a part in the drama. But, at every fateful moment, he is somewhere at hand, doing nothing himself but apparently there to observe that whatever should be done is done. He is the end of things, the conclusion, expected or unexpected; he is Fate.

He represents also the fickleness of Fate, and this was the function of the king's fool of the middle ages: he was there to remind his master that kings are but men, and that their deaths are as untimely and as inevitable as any other's. The fool was a privileged person, and (in theory, at least) whatever he chose to do went unpunished; a tradition that derived from the saturnalia of Roman times and, perhaps, from even older days, when a young man would be chosen for sacrifice at the year's end and would be allowed to behave exactly as he wished until the day he was to die. The Fool is the only card of the Major Arcana to survive in the modern pack of playing cards; he is the Joker, the card which can be used in place of any other in the pack.

And he is also the Fool of God, the shaman entranced with the wonders of the universe, the holy madman who lives a charmed life. He represents the best of luck – but it *is* luck, and likely to turn at any moment. When the Fool appears in a spread of Tarot cards, tread carefully: *he* may escape the snapping jaws of the dog behind and the crocodile in front, but will *you*?

Card	Gods, goddesses, mythical beings	Interpretation
Magician	Hermes/Mercury/Tehuti	Man in search of knowledge; the answer he seeks
Woman Pope	Hera/Juno Isis	Intuition, inspiration; the subconscious memory; lack of foresight
Empress	Demeter/Ceres Ishtar	Human understanding, femininity, sensuality, beauty and happiness
Emperor	Dionysos	Masculinity, independence, creativity, action
Pope	Zeus/Jupiter Serapis	Advice; justice; healing
Lovers	Cupid Venus/Aphrodite Paris	Choice, decision
Chariot	Mars	Achievement, success; danger of defeat
Justice	Themis	Caution in taking advice; control of one's fate
Hermit	Kronos/Saturn	Time; wisdom; withdrawal
Wheel of Fortune	Midas	Change; prudence; the eternal return
Fortitude	Cyrene Hercules/Samson	Strength of purpose; coming danger
Hanged Man	Attis Odin Christ Proteus	Adaptability; desire to learn; violent change and sacrifice
Death	Uranus Orpheus	Change by transformation, rebirth
Temperance	Iris (Ganymede)	Moderation, mercy; modification
Devil	Typhon/Set Kernunnos Zervan	The adversary; caution
The Tower	Babel Sodom Adam and Eve	Punishment; pride; divine inspiration
The Stars	Anahita/Inanna/Aphrodite/Venus	New beginning; pleasure; salvation
The Moon	Diana	Uncertainty; changeability
The Sun	Shamash/Apollo Circe	Splendour, health, wealth, affection; treachery
Judgment		Punishment or reward; final achievement
The World	Shamash Sin Nergal Ningirsu	Fulfilment, completion on a material level
The Fool		Fate; luck; the end

Some other Tarot packs

JUDGMENT

THE MAGICIAN

THE FOOL

LA MOUR

LE·DIABLE

ROUE DE FORTUNE

L'EMPEREUR

Although a wide range of Tarot card designs have been featured on the previous pages, there is a considerable number of other packs available, either revived from traditional designs or newly-drawn.

Top left: Judgment, the Magician and the Fool, from the 'Tarot Classic' pack printed by Müller for US Games Systems. This pack is based upon original woodcuts by Burdel dating from 1751, and is fully described in *Tarot Classic* by Stuart R. Kaplan. It will be seen that in style it is very similar to the 'Marseilles' pack of Grimaud. *Centre left*: the Lovers, the Devil, the Wheel of Fortune and the Emperor, from an eighteenth century Belgian pack recently re-published in facsimile.
Bottom left: the Lovers, the Magician, Temperance and the Moon, from the 63-card 'Bolognese' Tarot published by Viassone of Turin. *This page*: two contemporary designs. *Right*: the Moon, the Chariot, the Fool and the Queen of Swords from the 'Gypsy Tarot' designed by Walter Wegmüller, published by Sphinx Verlag, and described by Sergius Golowin in *Die Welt des Tarot*. *Below*: the Tower, the Woman Pope, Death and the Hermit from the pack designed by David Sheridan, which is described in full in *The Tarot* by Alfred Douglas

THE TOWER

THE PAPESS

DEATH

THE HERMIT

5
The significance of the minor arcana

ROI DE DENIER

REINE DE DENIER

VALET DES ÉPÉES

Above: three court or 'coat' cards from the Minor Arcana of the Müller 1JJ pack: the King of Cups, the Queen of Coins and the Jack of Swords

We have discussed in detail the significance of the Tarot trumps – the major arcana: they comprise a set of very powerful medieval symbols, as we have seen, with their roots in ancient history. You need only a short acquaintance with them to begin to discover what particular meaning they have for you; and from this point it is easy to use them for divination. But the minor arcana – substantially, almost identical with an ordinary pack of cards – are a very different matter. Of the fourteen cards of any one suit, nine (from two to ten) differ only in the number of suit symbols per card; and between the court cards and aces of the different suits, the differences are of degree rather than of kind. The novice, attempting to attribute a different significance to each card, has very little to guide him.

When you come to practise divination by cards by one of the methods described in the following chapter, it is only important that you know what each card means for you. Eventually you must make this interpretation for yourself on the basis of experience, but in the meantime it helps to know what significance is attached to each card by tradition. In many packs designed in the twentieth century, considerable attention has been paid to the minor arcana,

making each card clearly distinguishable and so more easily given an individual interpretation, but in traditional packs there is no sign of this. You will find, therefore, that many different meanings are attributed to these cards, and it is only possible here to give you the most traditional interpretation, applicable also to 52-card packs.

In the following chapter, the methods of divination first described are those making use only of the major arcana. When you have some experience you can go on to the more complex methods, and you will then need to know the interpretations below.

Cups, chalices, hearts
Ace: the home and domestic happiness. The meaning will be modified by other associated cards, so that we may find visitors to the house, change of residence, domestic quarrels, or feasts and parties.
Two: Success and good fortune; but care and attention will be necessary to secure it.
Three: Imprudence: impetuous decisions threaten favourable undertakings.
Four: A person not easily won: a bachelor or spinster, or a marriage delayed.
Five: Jealousy without foundation; or inability to make up one's mind, resulting in delay and avoidance of responsibility.

Six: A sign of credulity. You may be easily imposed upon, particularly by untrustworthy associates.

Seven: Fickleness and broken promises. Be on your guard against over-optimistic friends or thoughtless acquaintances.

Eight: Pleasurable company and good-fellowship; parties and planned celebrations.

Nine: The fulfilment of dreams and desires; good fortune and wealth.

Ten: Happiness in the family, perhaps unexpected success or good news.

Valet, Knave or 'Jack': A close friend; not always contemporary, for it may signify a long-lost childhood friend or sweetheart.

Knight: A false friend, a stranger from far away, a seducer; passing fate, to be seized before it vanishes again.

Queen: A faithful, loving woman, gentle and pleasing.

King: An honest and well-intentioned man, but hasty in his decisions and therefore not one to be relied upon for advice.

Rods, batons, clubs

Ace: Wealth and professional success; life-long friends and peace of mind.

Two: Disappointment and opposition from friends or business partners.

Three: A sign of more than one marriage; it may also be interpreted as a long engagement to one person, followed by a sudden marriage to someone else.

Four: Beware the failure of a project, which may result in financial loss, or itself be due to lack of money. False or unreliable friends play a part.

Five: Marriage with a wealthy woman.

Six: Profitable business in partnership.

Seven: Good fortune and happiness, but beware someone of the opposite sex.

Eight: Covetousness: someone is likely to make use of money that is not his own.

Nine: Disputes with friends; obstinate quarrels.

Ten: Unexpected good fortune, the cause or outcome of a long journey; but it may be accompanied by the loss of a dear friend.

Valet, Knave or 'Jack': A sincere but impatient friend; well-meaning flattery.

Knight: Providential help from a friend of the family; support from an unfamiliar source.

Queen: An affectionate and kindly woman, although inclined to be temperamental.

King: An honest and sincere man, generous and faithful.

Swords, spades

Ace: Misfortune, bad news, tidings of death; spiteful emotions.

Two: Change, removal, loss of home, separation.

Three: A journey, misfortune in love or marriage.

Four: Sickness, financial embarrassment, jealousy – all sorts of minor misfortunes which will delay any project in hand.

Five: Success in business, harmony in partnerships – but only after obstacles have been overcome. Beware ill-temper and discouragement.

Six: Only perseverance will enable you to bring your plans to fruition.

Seven: Quarrels with friends, and many troubles as a result.

Eight: Be cautious in all your undertakings: those who seem to be your friends may be revealed as rivals.

Nine: Reputedly the most ominous card of all: it may signify sickness, misfortune, all kinds of unhappiness.

Below: from an Italian double-headed pack: King of Swords, Queen of Rods and King of Cups

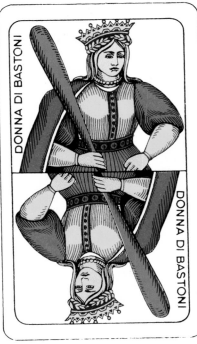

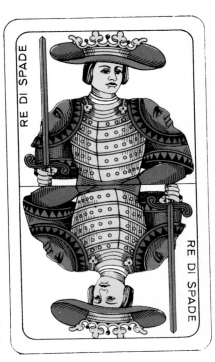

The significance of the minor arcana

KING of PENTACLES. KING of SWORDS. QUEEN of SWORDS.

Above: six court cards from the pack designed by A. E. Waite and executed by Pamela Coleman Smith. Every single card of the minor arcana has a distinctive design. *Below*: six court cards from the 'Ancien Tarot de Marseille' of Grimaud

Ten: Another ominous card: grief, imprisonment or, at the very least, the negation of all good indications.

Valet, Knave or 'Jack': A lazy or envious person, a hindrance in any undertaking, or perhaps an impostor, even a spy.

Knight: Romantic chivalry, inclined to extravagance, but brave and enterprising.

Queen: Treachery, betrayal, malice; a widow or a deserted person.

King: A man whose ambition over-rides everything.

Coins, pentacles, diamonds

Ace: An important message, or perhaps a valuable gift.

Two: A passionate love affair, but opposed by friends.

Three: Quarrels, lawsuits and domestic disagreements.

Four: Unhappiness arising from neglected or unfaithful friends; perhaps a secret betrayed.

Five: Unexpected news; its outcome may well be business success, realisation of an

THE KNAVE OF SWORDS THE KNIGHT OF SWORDS THE QUEEN OF CUPS

KNIGHT of WANDS.

QUEEN of WANDS.

KING of CUPS.

ambition, or a contented marriage.

Six: Early marriage – but also an early end to the marriage, and bad indications for a second.

Seven: Lies, rumours, unkind criticism; an unlucky gambler.

Eight: A marriage late in life; perhaps a journey; quite possibly a combination of the two.

Nine: A compulsion to travel, a taste for adventure, the desire to see changes in one's life.

Ten: Above all else, this card means money – but as the objective, not necessarily as the result, of your activities.

Valet, Knave or 'Jack': A selfish or jealous relative, or a messenger bringing unwelcome news.

Knight: A patient and persevering man; an inventor or discoverer.

Queen: A coquettish woman, given to interfering in others' affairs; scandal and rumour.

King: A hot-tempered, obstinate and vengeful man, dangerous when crossed.

THE KING OF MONEY

THE QUEEN OF MONEY

THE KNIGHT OF CLUBS

6
Divination by the Tarot

This is not the place to enter into a discussion concerning fate: whether events are pre-ordained, and what (if anything) one can do to change one's destiny. Think of yourself as an astronaut, fired from Cape Kennedy in a spaceship at the time of your birth. At Mission Control in Houston, every factor controlling your flight has been calculated before lift-off; it is possible for every adjustment to be made before your flight so that, if nothing goes wrong – and if, above all, you do nothing at all – the spaceship will automatically carry you to your destination. But sometimes things do go wrong: there is a minor interruption in the fuel feed, a solar cell does not charge properly, an electrical connection comes loose. And you, bored with your cramped surroundings, may begin to interfere with the operation of the ship. It may be no more than a movement of your body which changes the trim of the craft, or perhaps you decide to tinker with the switches. In Houston, minute changes in the flight of the spaceship will be detected a long time before you become aware of them, and instructions can be radioed to you to correct for them.

The astrologer, the crystal-gazer or the Tarot card reader can all be likened to Mission Control. By some psychic process they become aware of your original 'flight plan' and of the deviations that you are making from it. They can warn you of the changes you will have to make to avoid disaster. The horoscope, the pattern of the cards, or the crystal itself, all provide a focus of concentration which helps them to 'tune in' to you.

Even if you cannot accept the suggestion that such a flight plan exists – if you believe that your flight through space and time began as an accident – you are yourself aware of your flight, and of what you are doing to control it; the psychic adviser, like an experienced flight engineer, can warn you of the probable outcome of your actions. This is the significance and value of 'divination'.

Tarot cards present us with one of the most flexible and useful methods of seeking advice concerning what the future may hold in store. A number of cards are selected, and laid out in a particular pattern and order.

The Tarot cards must be read like the pages of a picture book. If we take only the 22 trumps, they can be arranged in 1,124,727,000,777,607,680,000 different sequences; add to this the incalculable number of groups of two, three, four or more and you will see that a selection of these trumps can portray every conceivable situation – and there are still 56 cards which have not entered into the calculation!

But how can we arrange it so that the group of cards we choose represents the situation we want it to? Some psychic researchers believe that even a completely random selection of cards, picked for instance by a sophisticated electronic machine, can be influenced by human beliefs and desires, but there is no need for us to go as far as this – and few people could afford such a machine in any case. Dealing out the cards by hand, and then selecting some of them, is a sufficiently effective method.

The important thing is to place yourself in as intimate a relationship with the cards as you can manage, without being consciously aware of what cards you are selecting. By concentrating all your mind upon the problem on which you are seeking advice, and by making a deliberate choice of a group of cards, but *without seeing their faces*, you will bring your psychic abilities into play so that, when you turn them over, you will be finely tuned to interpret their significance.

Take the 22 trumps face upward, and sort through them until you find a card which represents for you the situation on which you are seeking guidance. Then place the remaining cards face downward in a single pack and shuffle them as often as you wish. Remember to turn the cards as you cut them, so that some will be reversed. Then deal them out into three piles, putting each card on to whichever pile you think right – there is no need for each pile to contain the same number of cards, but it is probable that each will consist of between five and nine cards. Finally, concentrate very hard and choose one of the piles. Remember always to keep the cards the same way up as that in which you originally dealt them.

On a sheet of paper you should have made a little sketch to remind you of the way in which you are going to 'read' the cards. For instance, after placing the card that you first selected to represent the situation – the 'significator' – face upward on the table, you may decide to deal two cards (or one, or three) to its right to represent the events leading to this situation, two to its left to represent the future trend if you make no changes, two or three below to represent adverse influences, and the rest above to indicate the action you should take. You can deal the cards straight off the top of the pile you have chosen into their appropriate positions, or you can introduce a further element of choice by dealing them face downward, in the order you *feel* is right, before turning them over – but it is essential that you know what each card is to represent as you do this, and that is why you should keep the sketch of the layout beside you. After a little practice, you will no longer need this sketch and, like a child who has learnt to read, you will instinctively place the cards in the correct order as you lay them out one by one on the table before you.

Let us look at one or two examples and study how they may be interpreted. Experienced practitioners recommend that one should not read cards for oneself – it is considered too dangerous – but for the beginner there is no other way to obtain experience and understanding. If there is someone very near and dear to you who will give you their full sympathy, then it is best to practise with their help, but if, as is most likely, you are compelled to spend most of your study time by yourself, try not to seek advice on subjects that are of critical importance. Your problems must be serious ones, because consulting the Tarot cards is not a game, but to begin with let them be ones in which you can make mistakes without harm: deciding on a family outing, what new clothes to buy, or whether to renew an old acquaintanceship, for example. In this way you will be able to test the interpretation you have made, and so learn by your experience.

Example I

A young and unmarried woman has reached a critical point in her life: should she continue to develop her career, or should she accept the inevitable disruption of that career which will follow marriage? She is deeply in love with a man older than herself; this is not her first love affair, and she is confident that this is the man she would like to marry.

Because this is a matter of deciding between two well-defined alternatives, she chooses the Lovers as the significator. The selected pile of cards, when it is dealt out, contains eight cards, and it is remarkable that seven of these are reversed. Only the Woman Pope is unreversed, suggesting that the young woman should follow the dictates of her head rather than of her heart. To the right of the significator we find the Hermit, reversed, and the Sun, also reversed: the former obviously represents the older man, and the appearance of these two cards, both reversed, could indicate that the young woman is subconsciously not nearly so confident about her love as she would have us believe. But the reversed Hermit also signifies a lack of objectivity, and the reversed Sun suggests deceit; perhaps the man himself is not entirely faithful to the woman.

To the left of the significator, the reversed Empress together with the reversed Moon would imply strongly that, if the woman continues in her present course, letting her heart rule her head, her future will be a very uncertain one. As we have already noted, the Woman Pope is the dominant card in this spread, representing feminine intuition; the reversed Magician above can be read as suggesting that it is better for the woman to remain in her present state, even if it seems to hold out little promise of excitement in the near future, rather than take a step that she will later regret.

Below the significator, the combination of reversed Pope and reversed Justice represent bad advice of which the woman should be extremely wary.

This spread of cards and its interpretation is particularly interesting in that it has not directly answered the question that was asked. The young woman has been warned that her lover may not be all that he seems, and advised that it would be better not to change her present condition, but she has not been told that following a career will necessarily be her best course in the long run. And the Tarot, like all systems of divination, is mischievous: slyly these cards suggest that perhaps the advice they have given should be looked at more closely, and carefully weighed before any irrevocable decision is taken.

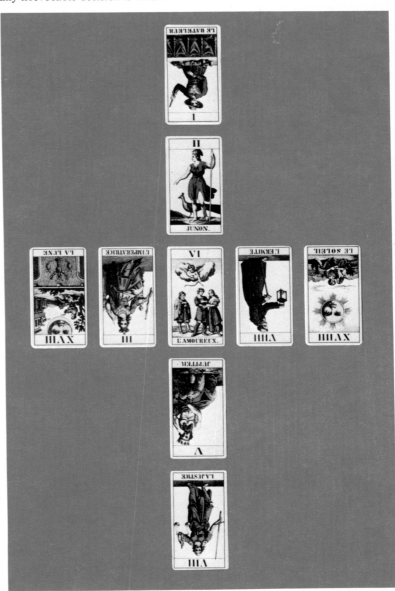

Example II
An elderly father is considering making over his estate to his son many years before his expected death: he is very concerned to discover whether he will continue to be properly looked after.

Although tempted to select the Hermit as significator, the questioner quite rightly chooses the Emperor, which properly represents him as a man still in possession of power and wealth. The selected pile dealt out is found to contain only seven cards.

To the right of the significator is the Sun reversed, which represents the events leading to the present situation. The questioner's physical powers are declining; it may transpire that there are several children between whom he has to decide – which of them will look after him best? To the left, the Lovers reversed, coupled with the Pope, suggest that the likely outcome of any request for advice is going to be of little value, since preservation of the status quo is probably the best course; this is reinforced by the cards below the significator, where the Judgment, counselling caution, is paired with the Devil reversed, suggesting that the questioner has really very little to worry about. The two cards above the significator, Death and the Fool, tell the questioner that he should continue to control his own destiny, and should not put his fate in the hands of another.

This particular spread of cards also does not directly answer the question asked, but in this case the interpretation provides rather more advice than was sought. The questioner learns that his powers of decision-making are unimpaired, and he is warned only that he should take good care before committing himself irrevocably. The cards also suggest that, if he has more than one child, it might be worthwhile consulting the Tarot on which is the most likely to handle his estate properly and look after him well in old age.

These two examples suffice to show how this very simple layout of cards may be used for practice in divination while you are learning to recognise and interpret the individual cards. Over the years, many authors have devised all sorts of complicated spreads, some of which we will now investigate. For the first few examples, we will continue to restrict ourselves to the Major Arcana, but for any spread it is, of course, possible to utilise any of the 78 cards of the pack. Later examples will show how most, or indeed all, of the pack may be used. We will assume that you have reached sufficient proficiency to be able to read the cards for someone other than yourself: it is now most important that all the shuffling and cutting of the pack should be done by the questioner. He or she should have a particular question in mind, and concentrate upon it, as this shuffling and cutting is carried out.

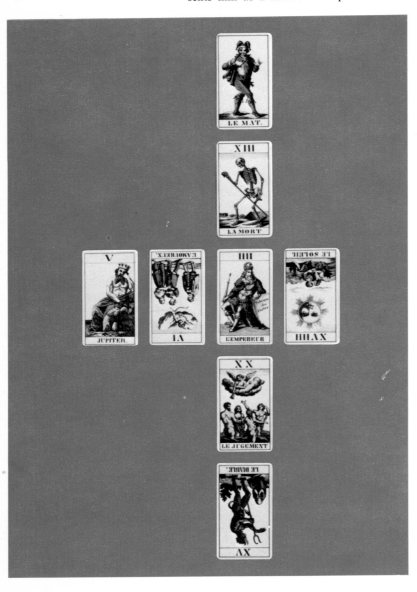

The 'Celtic' Cross

In consultation with the questioner, select one of the Tarot trumps to be the significator, and place it face upward on the table in front of you. Then get the questioner to shuffle the remaining 21 cards as often as he or she likes, cut them, and place them in a pile face down on the table some way to the left of the significator.

1. Turn over the first card (from left to right, so that it continues to point in the same direction, upright or reversed, as placed by the questioner). Place this card directly on top of the significator, saying 'This covers him (or her)'. This card represents the present atmosphere in which the questioner lives and works.

2. Turn over the second card and place it across the first, saying 'This crosses him'. This represents any immediate influences which may affect, or (in particular) conflict with, the interests of the questioner.

3. Turn over the third card, placing it above the first group of cards and saying 'This crowns him'. This represents the ultimate goal or destiny of the questioner; it may also represent his (or her) ideal aim in the subject under investigation.

4. Turn over the fourth card and place it below the central group, saying 'This is beneath him'. This represents the foundation of the question, the basic events and influences from the past which have brought about the identity and personality of the questioner.

5. Turn over the fifth card, placing it to the right of the central group, saying 'This is behind him'. It represents the recent past, and the effect it has had upon the present condition of the questioner.

6. Turn over the sixth card and place it to the left of the central group, saying 'This is before him'. This represents future influences that are likely to come into play in the near future.

These first six cards should now be interpreted, to show all the influences that will affect the answering of the question. Remember that your interpretation may sub-sequently be modified by the way in which you read the remaining cards, and that you are dealing only with the present condition of the questioner. Now you can proceed to deal with the specific enquiry made of the cards by the questioner. The last four cards are to be placed one above the other to the right of the cards already on the table.

7. Place the seventh card in position, saying 'This answers him'. This card represents the present position of the questioner, and may give directly the answer to the question. No final interpretation should be given, however, until all ten cards have been laid out and read.

8. The eighth card is placed above the seventh, with the words 'This strengthens him'. It represents people and factors which may have an effect upon the questioner.

9. The ninth card is placed above the eighth with the words 'This defines him'. It shows the inner feelings, emotions and intuitions of the questioner, and may also reveal secrets which the questioner is trying to keep concealed.

10. The tenth card is placed at the top of the right-hand row, with the words 'This ends it'. It reveals the end-result of everything represented by the preceding cards, and should be read as the conclusion of a continuous story which they tell.

Example III (see following page)

The questioner is a self-confident, capable mother of a family of three children. The two eldest have already left school; she finds herself with time on her hands, and is considering taking up a job. But the youngest child is still at school, and the mother is worried that this child may not yet be sufficiently mature, and may feel neglected if the mother goes out to work. What is the best thing to do?

The significator chosen here was the Empress, who was thought to represent most closely the situation of the questioner. The Woman Pope, dealt out as the first card to cover the Empress, confirms that this is indeed a question involving a woman, and the conflict that may arise between her material condition and her intuitive desires. It is particularly interesting that the second card, laid across the first, is its male counterpart, the Pope. The questioner has told us nothing about her husband, and his attitude to her problem; indeed, there is no way of telling whether he still lives with her, or is still alive – this card may even represent the youngest child about whom she is so concerned, or may suggest that the advice to be given her by you will conflict with her own desires. It is only when the full story is unrolled that the true significance of this card can be determined with confidence.

The third card, which crowns the group, is Justice, the card of decision: it tells us that the questioner hopes to receive carefully weighed advice upon which she can act immediately, but it also warns her that this is unlikely to be the case, and that she should consider the matter further before committing herself irrevocably. And the fourth card, the Magician, makes it clear that she alone must take responsibility for her decision, at the same time reinforcing your suspicion that a male influence is somewhere at work.

The fifth card, standing for the recent past, is the Hanged Man reversed. Right way up, this card symbolises a new understanding of what has gone before, and the likelihood of sudden change. Reversed, it suggests that the questioner has not learnt sufficient from past experiences, and indicates that perhaps she considered the same problem before, and rejected the step that she is now considering again. The sixth card, the Tower reversed, stands for the future, and adds to your understanding of the situation. The questioner is full of guilt because she wishes to do something that she thinks is likely to harm the structure of her family; but you can reassure her, telling her that her desire is a perfectly natural one. Nevertheless, it is one that is not likely to be fulfilled – at least, not as soon as she thinks.

So far, the first six cards have helped to throw light on the situation, giving a better understanding of the factors involved, and revealing certain aspects of the situation that the questioner kept hidden from you. The next four cards help you to answer her question, and give her the advice that she urgently desires.

The seventh card is the Fool, reversed. At the very point in the reading at which you expect the answer, there is no answer at all. Go carefully: Fate gives you a clear warning here, uncertainty piled upon uncertainty. Happily the eighth card is reassuring. Strength and resolve will come to the questioner's rescue; but she must use it with care and understanding, not seeking to impose her domination upon others weaker than herself.

The ninth card, the Devil reversed, shows that the questioner is herself aware that her strong personality can represent a danger to her family; but she can take heart, for her influence is a beneficial one. The last card is the Judgment, also reversed, and it tells you that no decision is a final one, that there is always an opportunity to redress a wrong and to admit honestly that one has made a mistake.

You can now ask the questioner about her husband; you may guess that he is still alive and with his family, but that he is a kindly, easygoing man who will support his wife in whatever course she decides upon. You can tell her that the decision she makes must be hers and hers alone, but that you think she is still not sufficiently sure about her situation and that of her child to make such a decision. She must look deeper into her motives and be sure that she is not letting selfish considerations over-rule her instincts as a mother and a wife. Then she can consult the Tarot again.

The Nine-Card Spread

Very similar to the Celtic Cross is the nine-card spread; it omits only card 2, which represents the immediate influences which may affect, or conflict with, the interests of the questioner. Interpretation of the other cards remains unchanged.

Example IV
The questioner is a middle-aged man, but still full of youth and enthusiasm. He has a good job, at which he works well, but he is dissatisfied with it. It does not give him sufficient opportunity to express his individuality and make use of the creative powers which he already feels weakening. Should he leave his present job and set up on his own account?

Here the significator agreed upon by the questioner is the Hermit, the elderly man setting out alone into the world in his search for truth.

The first card turned up indicates the present circumstances of the questioner: the Woman Pope, symbol of the desire to forsake rationality in favour of intuition, to give up the safe and mundane and embark upon a career that is more precarious but also more emotionally satisfying. And the second card, representing the questioner's ideal goal, is the Judgment, the card which itself means final achievement after difficulties.

The third card is the foundation of the question, and in this case it is the Magician, the man seeking an answer – the cards are stating the question so clearly that the questioner need not have said a word! The fourth card, to the right, represents the immediate past and the causes of the question: it is the Stars reversed. Right way up, this card represents rebirth and new beginning; reversed, it tells us that the questioner no longer finds in his present job any exciting hope for the future.

The last card in this group, the fifth card, reveals the probable future if current trends remain unchanged – what the questioner may expect if he does not make the break that he is contemplating. It is Death, reversed; it suggests that the questioner's gloomy view of his circumstances is largely justified. He can expect some gradual change, but neither for the better nor the worse, at least in a material sense; spiritually, he has little to look forward to but a gradual decline of his abilities over the coming years, until he reaches retirement.

Now we come to the four cards on the right. The reversed Pope says, in effect, 'Don't ask for advice, follow your instincts'. The Wheel of Fortune offers the desired change, but advises prudence; others are equally ambitious, and the questioner will have to compete with them. Fortitude, reversed, suggests that the questioner is subconsciously unconfident of his abilities, and

warns him that he needs more resolution if he is to succeed. But the Fool, striding happily into the unknown, crowns this spread of cards with encouragement. He is the youthful companion of the Hermit, the spirit of adventure, the young in heart upon whom the gods continue to smile. The dog, symbol of faithfulness, goes joyfully with him. The change that the questioner is considering is a dangerous one, and he could fail; but if he goes forward with confidence and determination, he will be undoubtedly a happier man.

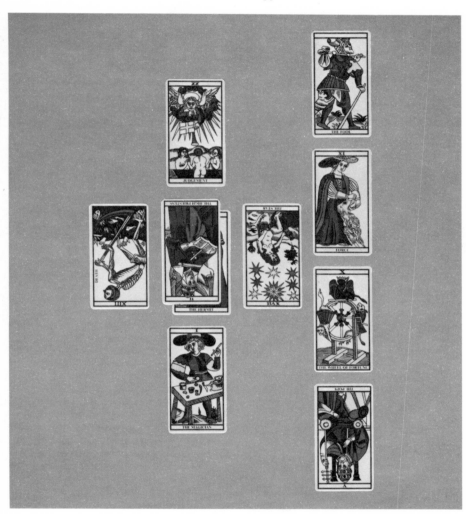

The Tree of the Qabala

The form of the sefirothic tree can be used, like the Celtic cross, as a pattern upon which to lay the cards and interpret them. The accompanying diagram shows how the ten sefiroth are related to each other. The tree is made up of three triangles, with the tenth sefiroth, Malkuth the Kingdom, below them. Each triangle contains two opposing concepts, and a third which reconciles them. Some qabalists have proposed an eleventh sefiroth, Daat, or Knowledge, and in this

position we may place the significator.

The Jewish mystics imagined themselves slowly ascending the tree from sefiroth to sefiroth; while they visualised inspiration as a 'lightning flash' which descended the tree by the same path, filling each sefiroth with its flow of energy. Tarot cards on the sefirothic tree should be read in the same way: as a slowly developing story from the bottom to the top, and then in a final vision of illumination from top to bottom.

Example V

The questioner is a woman at the crossroads of her life. Her husband has left her, leaving her pregnant, and she has begun divorce proceedings against him. She is deeply in love with a man who does not want children, and has asked her to go with him to a distant foreign country. She is being wooed by another man who would happily adopt the child when it is born. And she is also tempted to return to the career that she gave up for her first marriage.

It is very clear that one card above all others

is suitable as the significator: the Lovers, because it symbolises the difficulty of choice between several alternatives. Placed at the position of Daat, it completes the 'trunk' of the tree.

At the foot of the tree is the sefiroth of Malkuth, the Kingdom. This is of the earth most earthy, the purely material basis from which we begin our slow climb. Here the first card is the Empress, reversed: the body of woman, but sunk in idleness and sensuality. Above her lies Yesod, the Foundation, the public self, representing the emergence of individuality from the generality of Malkuth. This second card is the Chariot, also reversed. Our questioner finds great difficulty in expressing her individuality; she feels herself spiritually subjugated.

The next sefiroth is Hod, or splendour, representing the visible products of human activity, those things which people do by choice to show their awareness of spirituality. Here the Sun, again a reversed card, warns us that health and wealth must be struggled for, and there are many who will try to oppose our efforts. The questioner cannot expect anything to come easily.

The fourth card lies on Netsah, representing the enduring qualities, the instinctive aspects of creativity. The card is the Hanged Man, promising progression after sacrifice. Struggle against it as she will, the questioner knows in her heart that she must make that sacrifice, and that only good can come of it.

The fifth card lies on Tifereth, or beauty, the essential self, the silent 'watcher' of the balance between outward display of emotion and inner feeling. The questioner is represented in this sefiroth by the Wheel of Fortune, reversed: all about her is change, and there is a great danger that she will not act prudently, unable to reconcile the emotions that pull her one way and the other. For on Geburah, signifying power and good judgment, the Stars are also reversed; and on Hesed – love, mercy, the inner emotions – stands Death. The emotions she directs towards others are misplaced, and there is little hope of a satisfactory outcome; and her inner feelings must undergo a complete change. Somehow or other she must give up something that she loves.

We come now to the last three cards, representing the highest qualities of the intellect. The eighth card is on Binah, which is understanding, and the ninth on Hokmah, which is wisdom. Justice is the eighth card; the questioner has a good brain, which she should use to its full; but she must beware of narrow-mindedness and bigotry. Fortitude is reversed as the ninth card: she lacks resolve, letting those emotions that we have seen to be in such a turmoil obstruct her in doing what she knows in her heart to be right. At the head of the tree is Kether, the Supreme Crown; the reversed Pope tells her that the advice she is to be given is not the advice she expects.

The slow, analytical ascent of the tree is

complete; now you must make the synthesis, the sudden downward flash of inspiration. There is only one course for the questioner to follow: she must give up all that she thinks she loves, not only the man but the child as well. Only sacrifice and purgation, physical as well as spiritual, will bring her eventual contentment. The Wheel of Fortune at the centre of the tree will turn again, and perhaps the whole tree with it.

Turn the whole arrangement of the cards up the other way and study it again. Now the significator is the Chariot, standing for success; the Pope, representing justice and redemption, rules in the Kingdom. Yesod is the Lovers reversed: the choice has been made, the alternatives rejected. In Hod, the splendour of men's works, Fortitude stands supreme; and in Netsah the scales of blind chance have been tilted firmly for ever. Death, reversed, is now Geburah, for the change has cleared away all the old emotions; and the Stars of hope shine out, promising love and mercy in Hesed. The Hanged Man, Death's companion, is reversed in Binah; and the Sun in all his glory fills Hokmah, the sefiroth of wisdom. Crowning all is the Empress, the true feminine principle.

So much for methods of laying out cards using only the Tarot trumps; now let us take a look at various schemes that make use of the full pack of cards. One of the simplest of these is that given by Papus in *The Tarot of the Bohemians*.

The Method of Papus

Papus's 'Rapid Process'
1. Select from the minor arcana the suit that refers to the kind of advice required: Rods for business matters, Cups for affairs of the heart, Swords for legal questions or a dispute of any kind, and Discs for money matters.
2. Shuffle this suit, and ask the questioner to cut them.
3. Take the first four cards from the top of the pack and, without looking at them, arrange them in a cross as shown on the right.
4. Take the major arcana, shuffle, and have them cut for you as before.
5. Ask the questioner to take out seven cards

from the major arcana **without** looking at them, and shuffle them.
6. Ask the questioner to cut the pile of seven cards, and then take the top three and lay them face down as indicated in the diagram on the left.

Read the cards as follows: 1 represents the *commencement*, 2 the *apogee*, 3 the *obstacles*, and 4 the *fall*; I represents the influences that have affected the matter in the past, II indicates the influences of the present, and III shows what will affect and determine the future.

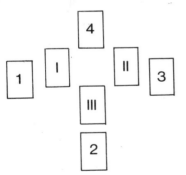

Papus's 'More Elaborate Process'
1. Shuffle all the minor arcana together, and have the questioner cut them.
2. Take the first twelve cards from the pack, laying them out in a circle.
3. Shuffle the major arcana, have them cut by the questioner, and get him to choose seven cards.
4. Place the first four in a smaller circle within the first circle, opposite numbers 1, 10, 7 and 4 respectively, in that order. Lay the remaining three cards as a triangle within this circle, so that the final arrangement is:

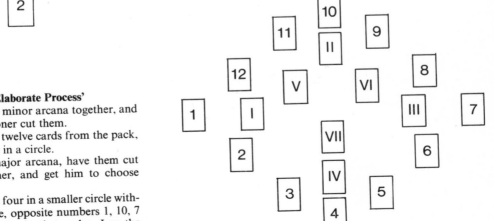

The twelve minor arcana represent progressive phases of the event during the development represented by I, the commencement, II, the apogee, III, the decline or obstacle, IV, the fall. Cards V, VI, and VII represent respectively the past, present and future.

The Horsehoe Spread

This method gives a straightforward answer to a specific question.

After having shuffled the complete pack, major and minor arcana together, ask the questioner to cut them. Then take the first seven cards from the top of the pack, and lay them face upward in the following order, taking care not to reverse the cards as you do so.

Card 1 refers to influences in the past.
Card 2 indicates the present circumstances of the questioner.
Card 3 reveals the future in general terms.
Card 4 indicates the recommended course for the questioner to take.
Card 5 reveals the attitudes of those surrounding the questioner.
Card 6 indicates obstacles that may stand in the way.
Card 7 suggests the probable final outcome of the problem.

Example VI

A young man, who has taken over the flat of a friend, to whom he is paying a rent, is being threatened with eviction by his landlady because the friend is behindhand with payments on the lease. What will be the outcome?

The first card, which represents past influences, is the Three of Cups reversed, revealing that what might seem to be an imprudent undertaking (becoming the sub-tenant of a friend who is unreliable) was in reality a sensible step. But the second card, indicating present circumstances, is the Seven of Swords, symbolising a quarrel involving the friend.

The third card, which reveals the general nature of what is to come, is the Emperor reversed, suggesting that legal power will be dissipated in fruitless activity.

The fourth card, the Wheel of Fortune reversed, advises the questioner to do nothing: he should accept change if it comes and not act impetuously without wisdom.

The fifth card, standing for the attitudes of those associated with the questioner, is the Six of Rods, signifying profitable partnership; and Temperance in the sixth position suggests that few obstacles stand in his way. Finally, the seventh card, the probable final outcome, is the Queen of Cups reversed. This tells us that a quarrelsome woman will be thwarted in her attempts to provoke discord.

The meaning of this card reading is clear: the young man should remain patient, because his friend will not desert him. The rent will be paid, and the landlady will not succeed in her plan to evict him.

The 'Italian' Method

Here is another method, the Italian, which is said to correspond most nearly to the original method of divining with the Tarot.
1. Shuffle, cut, spread out the whole pack face downwards. Have 22 cards drawn and spread them before you as they are drawn, from the left to the right in three series of seven plus one.

The first seven give general information as to the immediate past.

The second seven relate to the present, and especially to the actual anxieties of the client.

The third seven deal with the immediate future, and the remaining card indicates the final resolution.

2. Connect the separate meanings of the cards in fives (counting so that there are three cards between every two consulted), starting from the first on the left.

3. Reshuffle the whole pack, have it cut and 48 cards drawn which are made up into 12 packs of 4 each, the meaning of each being:

I. The personality of the client
II. Money matters
III. Family relations
IV. Parents (father, mother and their property)
V. Pleasures, personal satisfaction
VI. Colleagues, collaborators, current relations
VII. Marriage, lawsuits
VIII. Health
IX. Personal merits and their results
X. Actual good or bad luck
XI. Assistance and protection
XII. Unpleasantnesses and misfortunes

4. If it is desired to be more precise, reshuffle, cut and have 15 cards drawn which are spread out from left to right, then 15 more, which are placed in a stack on one side.

Start the interpretation again, beginning with the first card on the left, in fives as before.

Then give the stack of 15 to the questioner, asking him to draw one which he will place on that card spread out which interests him most. This gives the supreme enlightenment.

The Methods of Macgregor Mathers

In his slim volume on the Tarot, Macgregor Mathers outlined three methods of increasing complexity, which will be described in succession.

First method

The full pack of seventy-eight cards having been shuffled and cut, deal the top card on a part of the table which we will call B, the second card on another place which we will call A. (These will form the commencement of two heaps, A and B, into which the whole pack is to be dealt.) Then deal the third and fourth cards on B, and the fifth on A; the sixth and seventh on B, and the eighth on A; the ninth and tenth on B, and the eleventh on A. Continue this operation of dealing two cards on B and one on A, till you come to the end of the pack. A will then consist of twenty-six cards, and B of fifty-two.

Now take up the B heap of fifty-two cards. Deal the top card on a fresh place which we will call D, and the second card on another place C. (This will form the beginning of two fresh heaps, C and D.) Then deal the third and fourth cards on D, and the fifth on C; the sixth and seventh on D, and the eighth on C, and so on as before through these fifty-two cards. There will now be three heaps; A = 26 cards, C = 17 cards, and D = 35 cards.

Again take up the heap D of 35 cards, and deal the top card on a fresh spot F, and the second card on another place E (so as to make two fresh heaps E and F). Now deal the third and fourth cards on F and the fifth on E, and so on as before through these 35.

There will now be four heaps altogether. A = 26 cards, C = 17 cards, E = 11, and F = 24. Put F aside altogether, as these cards are not to be used in the reading, and are supposed to have no bearing on the question.

Take A and arrange the 26 cards face upwards from right to left (being careful not to alter the order), so that they are in the form of a horseshoe, the top card being at the low-

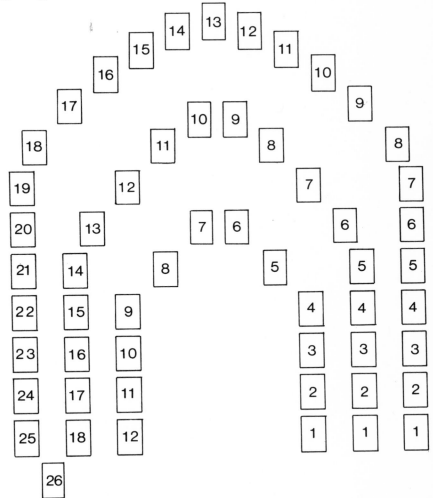

est right-hand corner, and the 26th at the lowest left-hand corner. Read their meanings from right to left as before explained. When this is done so as to make a connected answer, take the 1st and 26th and read their combined meaning, then that of the 2nd and 25th,

Divination by the Tarot

and so on till you come to the last pair which will be the 13th and 14th. Put A aside, and take C and read it in exactly the same way, then E last.

This is a very ancient mode of reading the Tarot, and will be found reliable.

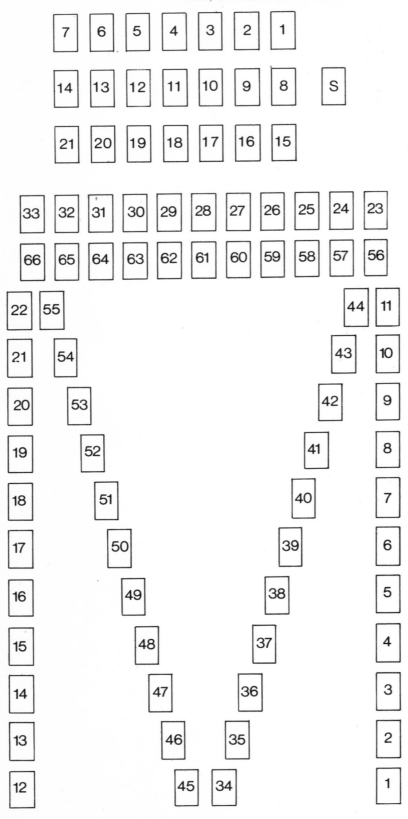

Second Method

Withdraw the card selected for the significator from the pack. Then shuffle and cut the same as before. Place the significator on the table face upwards, leaving plenty of room for the selected cards on the left-hand side of it. Now go carefully through the pack, taking the top card first, then the seventh card from it; and so on through the pack, recommencing if necessary, until you have drawn 21 cards by taking every seventh. Arrange these 21 cards in three rows of seven each, from right to left, on the left-hand side of the significator as indicated in the diagram on the left.

Read the meaning of each row from right to left, beginning with the significator; then combine the 1st and 21st, the 2nd and 20th, and so on, as in the previously described method.

Third Method

This mode of laying out the cards is rather more complicated than the preceding. Withdraw the significator, shuffle, and cut as before. Then deal as in the diagram, face upwards.

The cards will thus form a triangle within a species of arch; and the significator is to be placed in the centre of the triangle face upwards. The top card is to be dealt on number 1, the second card on number 2, the twelfth card on number 12 and so on up to number 66, when the remaining 11 cards are to be put aside and not used in the reading.

Then 1 to 11 and 34 to 44 inclusive will show the past: 23 to 33 and 56 to 66 inclusive will show the present: and 12 to 22 and 45 to 55 inclusive will show the future.

Now read them simply in order from 1 to 44 for the past, from 23 to 66 for the present, and from 12 to 55 for the future.

Then combine the significator with every two cards, S–34–1; S–33–2; S–32–3; and so on up to S–44–11, for the past. Then take S–56–23; S–57–24; and so on for the present. And then take S–45–12; S–46–13; up to S–55–22, for the future.

Again vary the combinations by taking S–44–1; S–43–2; up to S–34–11, for the past; S–66–23; S–65–24; up to S–56–33, for the present: and S–55–12; S–54–13; up to S–45–22, for the future.

Finally, combine them all together, 66–1; 65–2; 64–3, and so on up to 34–33; placing them in a single packet one on the other as you do so; and when this is finished, deal the whole 66 cards in one large circle, placing the significator as a starting-point, when 33 will be the first card and 66 the last card on either side of the significator. Now gather them up in pairs for the last reading S–66; 33–1; 34–2; and so on up to the last card, which will be a single one. Draw two other fresh cards at random from the 11 cards which have not been used in the reading, and place them face upwards one on either side to form a surprise. Read these three from right to left as conclusion.

The Royal Spread

This method requires 54 cards: the 22 trumps, the court cards, and the aces and cards numbered II, III and IV in each suit.

From these cards the questioner chooses five: one as his own significator, and four more to represent persons or events which are concerned with the question. These are laid out face up in the positions marked S, 1, 2, 3, 4 in the accompanying diagram. The remaining 49 cards are then shuffled and cut by the questioner, and are laid out, beginning at the top row, from right to left.

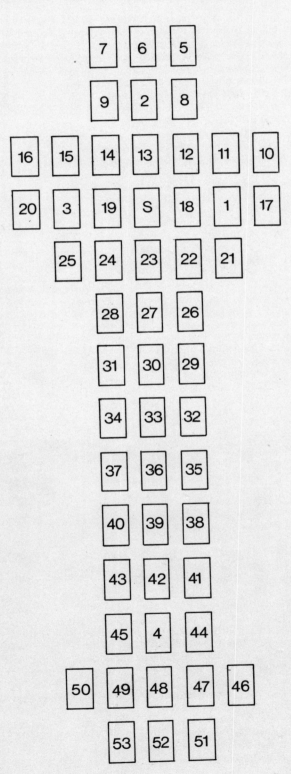

The Method of Aleister Crowley

Finally, here is the extremely long and complex method laid down by Aleister Crowley in his *Book of Thoth*.

1. Choose a card to represent the questioner, using your knowledge or judgment of his character rather than dwelling on his physical characteristics.

2. Take the cards in your left hand. In the right hand hold the wand over them and say: I invoke thee, I A O, that thou wilt send H R U, the great Angel that is set over the operations of this Secret Wisdom, to lay his hand invisibly upon these consecrated cards of art, that thereby we may obtain true knowledge of hidden things, to the glory of thine ineffable Name. Amen.

3. Hand the cards to questioner, and bid him think of the question attentively, and cut.

4. Take cards as cut, and hold as for dealing.

First operation: This shows the situation of the questioner at the time when he consults you.

1. The pack being in front of you, cut, and place the top half to the left.

2. Cut each pack again to the left.

3. These four stacks represent I H V H (Yod-Heh-Vau-Heh), from right to left.

4. Find the significator. If it be in the Yod pack, the question refers to work, business, etc.; if in the first Heh pack it relates to love, marriage, pleasure or sex; if in the Vau pack it relates to trouble, loss, scandal, quarrelling, etc.; if in the second Heh pack the question relates to money, goods, and such purely material matters.

5. Tell the questioner what he has come for: if he agrees proceed further, if wrong, abandon the divination.

6. If right, spread out the pack containing the significator, face upwards. Count the cards from him towards the left, including the significator as the first card.

   For Knights, Queens and Knights, count 4
   For Valets, count 7
   For Aces, count 11
   Small cards: as face value
   Trumps: Elemental: 3
          Planetary: 9
          Zodiacal: 12

The Elemental Trumps are: Fool, Hanged Man, and Judgment
The Planetary Trumps are: Magician, Woman Pope, Empress, Wheel of Fortune, Ruined Tower, Sun and World
The Zodiacal Trumps are: Emperor, Pope, Lovers, Chariot, Fortitude, Hermit, Justice, Death, Temperance, Devil, Stars and Moon

   Make a story of these cards. This story is that of the beginning of the affair.

7. Pair the cards on either side of the significator, then those outside them, and so on. Make another story which would fill in the details omitted in the first.

8. If this story is not quite accurate, do not be discouraged. Perhaps the questioner himself does not know everything. But the main lines ought to be laid down firmly, with correctness, or the divination should be abandoned.

Second operation: Development of the question.

1. Shuffle, invoke suitably, and let the questioner cut as before.

2. Deal cards into twelve stacks, for the twelve astrological houses of heaven.

3. Make up your mind in which stack you ought to find the significator, e.g. in the seventh house if the question concerns marriage, and so on.

   1. Life and Health
   2. Money
   3. Kindred and journeys
   4. Inheritance
   5. Children
   6. Sickness
   7. Marriage
   8. Death
   9. Long Journeys
   10. Honour
   11. Friends
   12. Enemies

4. Examine this chosen stack. If the significator is not there, try some cognate house. On a second failure, abandon the divination.

5. Read the stack, counting and pairing as before.

Third operation: Further development of the question.

1. Shuffle, etc., as before.

2. Deal cards into twelve stacks for the twelve signs of the zodiac.

3. Divine the proper stacks according to which of the signs would normally accommodate the question, e.g.:

   1. Aries: Anger
   2. Taurus: Beauty
   3. Gemini: Learning
   4. Cancer: Rest
   5. Leo: Prominence
   6. Virgo: Labour
   7. Libra: Affection
   8. Scorpio: Sexuality, birth, death, psychic areas, passion
   9. Sagittarius: Travel
   10. Capricorn: Old age, cold, responsibility
   11. Aquarius: Eccentricity, occultism
   12. Pisces: Sleep, mysticism, psychism

4. If the significator is not found after two tries, abandon the reading. If it is, then spread and read, pair and read again, as before.

Fourth operation: Penultimate aspects of the question.

1. Shuffle, etc, as before.

2. Find the significator and place him upon the table. The 36 cards which immediately follow him form this reading (the remaining

41 being set aside until the final step). Deal out the thirty-six cards in a wheel around him, beginning at 12 o'clock and proceeding in a counter-clockwise direction. Then count and read, pair and read as previously.

Fifth operation: Final result.
1. Take up the entire deck again, replacing the significator in it.
2. Shuffle, etc, as before.
3. Deal the cards into ten packs in the form of the Tree of Life, as on page 17.
The 11th card will then go on 1, 12 on 2, etc.
4. The positions with their correspondences are as follows:

Kether: The Crown. The Fool, Neptune, the highest internal quest

Hokmah: Wisdom. The intellect, the universe. Uranus, personal initiative

Binah: Understanding. Outer intellect, Death, Saturn, trouble.

Hesed: Mercy. Inner emotion, the Emperor, Jupiter, financial success, prosperity

Geburah: Judgment. Outer emotion, the Tower, Mars, enemies, wars, revenge

Tifereth: Beauty. The essential self, the Watcher, the Hanged Man, the Sun, splendour

Netsah: Eternity. Involuntary processes, the Empress, Venus, love, passion, sex

Hod: Reverberation, voluntary processes, the Magician, Mercury, wheeling and dealing, communications, politics

Yesod: Foundation. Personal Ego, the High Empress, the Moon, intuition and feelings, the soul

Malkuth: Kingdom. The body, the Wheel of Fortune, Pluto (?), the home, physical appetites
5. Locate the significator in one of the piles. Keep searching until you find it. Discard all the other stacks as they will not be needed. Spread out the stack.
6. Count and pair as before.

The Hierophant, trump number V, from the pack known as the *Book of Thoth*, designed by Aleister Crowley and executed for him by Frieda Harris

85

7
Astrology, alchemy and Tarot

As we have seen, astrological symbolism plays a part in the imagery of the Tarot, and it was of great importance in the various medieval memory systems. Several attempts have been made, therefore, to assign specific astrological identities to the different trumps.

The first problem is finding sufficient identities for the 22 cards. Classical astrology recognised only seven planets – the word comes from the Greek meaning 'wanderers', and comprises the sun, moon, Mercury, Venus, Mars, Jupiter and Saturn – and twelve signs of the zodiac. Knowing, as we do, that the Tarot trumps are only the remnants of the *tarocchi* which included all these identities, we would not expect it to be possible to attach astrological significance to each of the surviving Tarot cards, but let us see what can be done.

One so-called 'traditional' system assigns elements, planets and signs of the zodiac to the letters of the Hebrew alphabet as follows:

aleph	air	I
beth	Moon	II
gimel	Mars	III
daleth	Sun	IIII
he	Aries	V
vau	Taurus	VI
zain	Gemini	VII
heth	Cancer	VIII
tet	Leo	IX
yod	Virgo	X
kaph	Venus	XI
lamed	Libra	XII
mem	Water	XIII
nun	Scorpio	XIIII
samekh	Sagittarius	XV
ayin	Capricorn	XVI
pe	Mercury	XVII
tzaddi	Aquarius	XVIII
qoph	Pisces	XIX
resh	Saturn	XX
shin	Fire	XXI (or 0)
tau	Jupiter	XXII (or XXI)

Right: an alchemical drawing from John Dastin's fifteenth century manuscript, *De erroribus*, in the British Museum. This illustration contains elements very similar to those in the Tarot trumps of the Moon, the Sun, and the Last Judgment – but these must be regarded only as evidence of the widespread applicability of medieval imagery, since no other of the accompanying illustrations bears the faintest resemblance to a Tarot card

This is clearly unsatisfactory: Mars is associated with card VII, not III; Gemini with card XIX; Cancer with card XVIII – and so on. And what has become of the element Earth? In the classical tradition, three signs of the zodiac are connected with Earth, three with Fire, three with Water and three with Air, so the inclusion of the four (or, rather, three) elements seems completely unjustified.

Crowley's system, which is equally unsatisfactory, attempts to rearrange this order.

Above: an engraving from Thurneysser's *Quinta essentia* (1574) illustrates the relationship between the signs of the zodiac, the 'four humours' and various alchemical processes

Astrology, alchemy and Tarot

Following Macgregor Mathers, he found it necessary to interchange Justice and Fortitude, so that these cards are numbered respectively XI and VIII:

0	aleph	Air
I	beth	Mercury
II	gimel	Moon
III	daleth	Venus
IV	he	Aries
IV	vau	Taurus
VI	zain	Gemini
VII	heth	Cancer
VIII	tet	Leo
IX	yod	Virgo
X	kaph	Jupiter
XI	lamed	Libra
XII	mem	Water
XIII	nun	Scorpio
XIIII	samekh	Sagittarius
XV	ayin	Capricorn
XVI	pe	Mars
XVII	tzaddi	Aquarius
XVIII	qoph	Pisces
XIX	resh	Sun
XX	shin	Fire
XXI	tau	Saturn

One or two astrological subjects have been brought into a more satisfactory relationship with the images of the trumps, but just as many are as unrelated as ever. One of the problems is the continued insistence on keeping the signs of the zodiac in their normal order, another is the intrusion of three of the four elements.

Joseph Maxwell proposed a system which proved to be rather more logical. Astrological data include other figures beside the positions of the twelve parts of the zodiac and of the planets; there is the 'head of the dragon' and the 'tail of the dragon' – the points where the course of the moon crosses that of the sun – and also the 'part of fortune'. Surprisingly, Maxwell adopted only the dragon's head into his system, allocating no astrological significance to the Tower or the Fool:

I	Magician	Sun
II	Woman Pope	Moon
III	Empress	Venus
IIII	Emperor	Jupiter
V	Pope	Mercury
VI	Lovers	Sagittarius
VII	Chariot	Mars
VIII	Justice	Libra
IX	Hermit	Pisces
X	Wheel of Fortune	Capricorn
XI	Fortitude	Leo
XII	Hanged Man	Aries
XIII	Death	Saturn
XIIII	Temperance	Aquarius
XV	Devil	Dragon's Head
XVI	Tower	
XVII	Star	Taurus
XVIII	Moon	Cancer
XIX	Sun	Gemini
XX	Judgment	Scorpio
XXI	World	Virgo
0	Fool	

This makes good sense in many cases: the principal oddities are the assignment of Mercury to the Pope, Pisces to the Hermit, Taurus to the Star, and Scorpio to the Judgment; and there seems no good reason why the dragon's tail should not have been assigned to (say) the Tower. For those readers to whom a set of astrological relationships would be of help in interpreting the Tarot, the following scheme is offered:

I	Magician	Mercury
II	Woman Pope	Moon
III	Empress	Venus
IV	Emperor	Dragon's Head
V	Pope	Jupiter
VI	Lovers	Sagittarius
VII	Chariot	Mars
VIII	Justice	Libra
IX	Hermit	Saturn
X	Wheel of Fortune	Sun
XI	Fortitude	Leo
XII	Hanged Man	Aries
XIII	Death	Dragon's Tail
XIIII	Temperance	Aquarius
XV	Devil	Capricorn
XVI	Tower	Scorpio
XVII	Star	Virgo
XVIII	Moon	Cancer
XIX	Sun	Gemini
XX	Judgment	Pisces
XXI	World	Taurus
0	Fool	Part of Fortune

* * *

Another medieval study that made great use of symbolism was alchemy. A good proportion of this symbolism was astrological, but it was combined in many unexpected ways with other symbols taken from classical mythology, from religion, and from various natural sources – very much, indeed, in the same way as the medieval memory systems, which relied in part on the association of images, and in part on the incongruity of an unexpected image in an unexpected place.

Since both subjects derive their symbolism from the same source, it is not surprising that many of the same features occur in alchemy and in the Tarot; but the absence of most of the commonest alchemical symbols from the Tarot is more remarkable. There is no sign, for instance, of the red man and the white woman, the raven, the green lion, the grey wolf or the toad – all common in alchemical texts. Some excitement was caused by the observation that a drawing from a sixteenth-century manuscript in the British Museum, purporting to show an operation in the manufacture of the Philosophers' Stone, contained graphic elements very similar to those in the Moon, the Sun and the Judgment. Unfortunately, all the other drawings in the manuscript are clearly alchemical in content, and do not resemble Tarot cards at all. There seem to be no grounds whatsoever, despite the modifications made by Lévi to the card of the Devil, for supposing that the Tarot cards are in any way connected with alchemy.

Bibliography

Butler, Bill. *The Definitive Tarot*. Rider, London. 1975

Case, Paul Foster. *The Tarot: a Key to the Wisdom of the Ages*. Macoy Publishing Co, Virginia. 1947

Cavendish, Richard. *The Tarot*. Michael Joseph, London. 1975

Court de Gebelin, Antoine. *Monde Primitif*. Paris. 1775–1784

Crowley, Aleister. *The Book of Thoth*. Samuel Weiser, New York. 1969

D'Allemagne, Henry René. *Les Cartes à Jouer*. Hachette, Paris. 1906

Douglas, Alfred. *The Tarot*. Gollancz, London. 1973

Gettings, Fred. *The Book of Tarot*. Hamlyn, London. 1973

Gray, Eden. *The Tarot Revealed*. Inspiration House, New York. 1969

Haich, Elisabeth. *The Wisdom of the Tarot*. George Allen & Unwin, London. 1975

Huson, Paul. *The Devil's Picturebook*. Sphere Books, London. 1972

Kaplan, Stuart R. *Tarot Classic*. Robert Hale, London. 1974

Lèvi, Eliphas (Constant, Alphonse Louis). *Dogme et Rituel de la Haute Magie*. Paris. 1860

Mathers, S. L. Macgregor. *The Tarot*. London. 1888

Papus (Encausse, Gerard). *The Tarot of the Bohemians* (trans. A. E. Waite). Weiser, New York. 1969

Waite, Arthur Edward. *The Pictorial Key to the Tarot*. Rider, London. 1971

The Grimaud and Müller packs are distributed in Great Britain by Waddingtons Playing Card Co Ltd